WYVE

CW01237867

MICHAEL J. DOUST

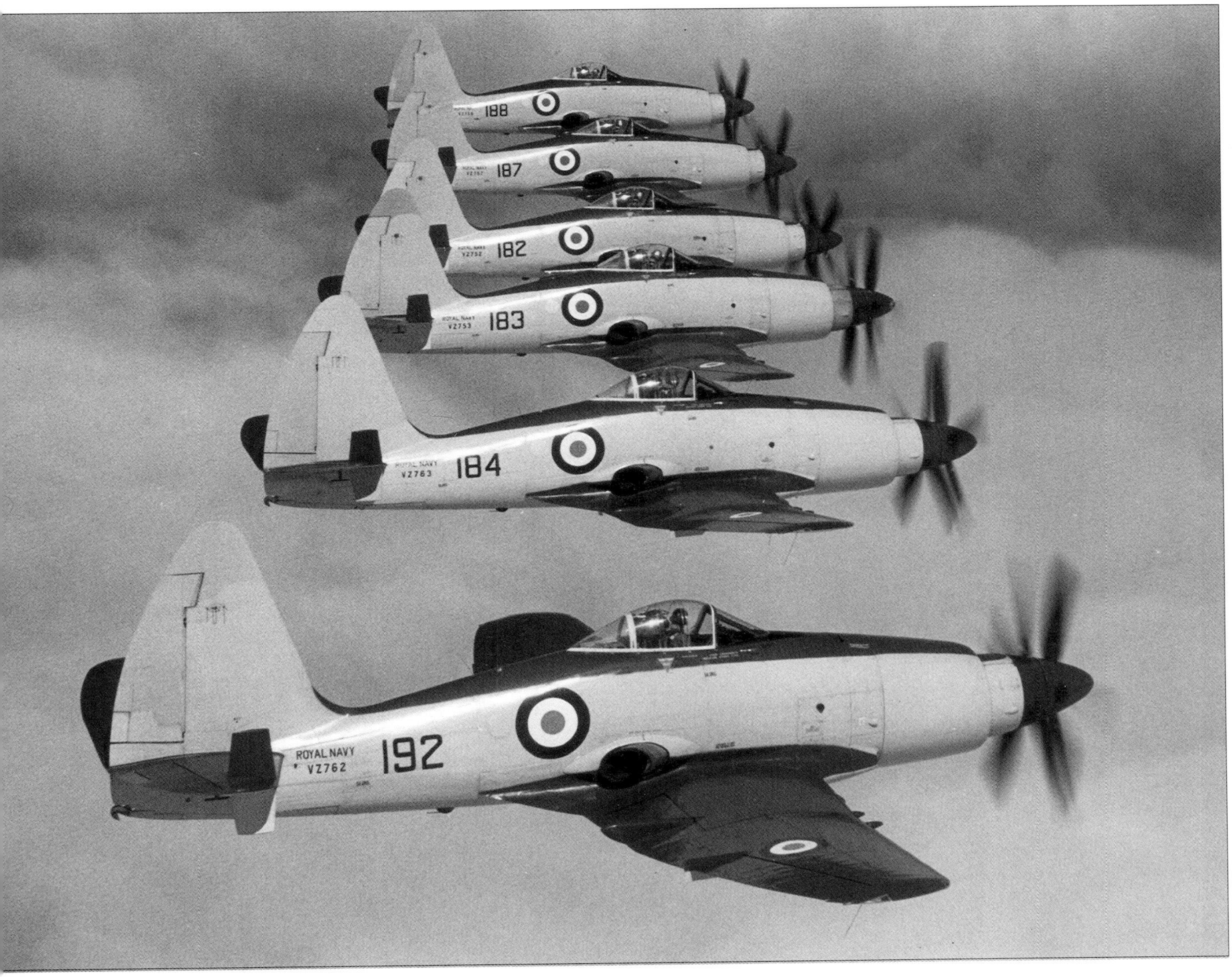

AD HOC PUBLICATIONS

FROM THE COCKPIT 1

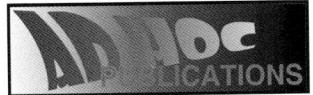

INTRODUCTION

THE Wyvern strike fighter was the last fixed-wing aircraft to be built by Westland and was something of an oddity. It had a comparatively short front-line service life—about five years only, from May 1953 to March 1958—and then went into storage, finally vanishing in various breakers' yards. In reality it was an interim aircraft, fulfilling a role as a stop-gap until the Scimitar and Buccaneer appeared on the scene. Had it not been for NATO's requirement for the Royal Navy to have two torpedo fighter squadrons, it would doubtless have been put to death during the feasibility studies.

It was a large and very heavy strike machine, and when alongside the Hawker Sea Hawk, its shipboard companion for much of its career, it looked positively enormous. For its size, the Wyvern had one of the largest tail *empennages* of any in service; even so, these flying and control surfaces had subsequently to be increased in area and otherwise modified in order to improve the aircraft's stability.

Of all military fighters currently in service at that time, the Wyvern was unique in being the only one fitted with a turbo-prop powerplant, and this drove the largest propellers then in use. The aircraft was

also capable of delivering a heavy conventional warload to any target with deadly effect. The torpedo delivery requirement was revoked in 1955, but the Wyvern remained a very effective minelayer.

The Wyvern did go to war during its short in-service period with the Royal Navy, being used in combat throughout the Suez Crisis. Although a couple of aircraft were lost to enemy anti-aircraft fire in these operations, both pilots managed to return close enough to their carrier to be rescued by SAR helicopter without injury.

With the disbandment of 831 Squadron late 1957, 813 Squadron soldiered on at RNAS Ford and aboard HMS *Eagle* as the last remaining front-line Wyvern unit, and this was finally disbanded during 1958. All the aircraft were flown to RNAS Lossiemouth (HMS *Fulmar*) in Morayshire, where they were placed in a reserve aircraft park. A year or so later they were towed away ignominiously, to be broken up by a local scrapyard dealer for £5 a ton. So ended the career of a powerful strike fighter that was enjoyed by all who flew and went to war in it.

WESTLAND WYVERN	
Manufacturer:	Westland Aircraft Company, Yeovil, Somerset, England.
Design:	Westland W.34.
Chief Designer:	John Wingfield-Digby, FRAeS.
Assistant Designer:	Fred Ballam, FRAeS.

Left: Wyvern S. Mk 4s of 813 and 827 Naval Air Squadrons ranged aft aboard HMS *Eagle*, June 1955. Further forward, abreast the island, are Sea Hawks.
Above: Wyvern S.4 WN334 of 831 NAS, photographed in early 1956 and toting 3-inch rocket projectiles beneath the wings.
Right: The aircraft the Wyvern was designed to replace—the Blackburn Firebrand torpedo bomber.

THREE

REQUIREMENT

NAVAL Staff Requirement N.11/44 called for a single-seat ship-based aircraft to replace the Blackburn Firebrand. The Royal Air Force had a similar project, F.13/44 (a replacement for the Bristol Beaufighter, which had taken over the ship-strike role of the Beaufort towards the end of World War II), and this could have been met by the Wyvern, but the RAF had quickly appreciated that any such dedicated maritime strike aircraft would have little chance of being able to deliver its weapons when confronted by modern shipboard defence systems and their requirement was cancelled. Nevertheless, the North Atlantic Treaty Organisation (NATO), which had been formed after the war as a counter to Soviet expansion, laid down a requirement for the Royal Navy to have at least two torpedo strike squadrons.

Westland Aircraft were tasked to satisfy the N.11/44 requirement. The specifications were demanding, and made more difficult by the selection of the 24-cylinder, sleeve-valve, Rolls-Royce Eagle to power the aircraft. The configuration of this engine, viewed head-on, resembled a capital 'H' on its side, and it was fitted with two contra-rotating, four-bladed propellers. However, it was also a requirement that the airframe be capable of accepting a turbo-prop powerplant, when such became available.

The Wyvern was a cantilever low-wing monoplane of all-metal, stressed-skin construction, fitted with retractable main and tail wheel landing gear plus catapult and holdback attachment points and a tail hook. It was to be capable of carrying four 20mm cannon in the wings, and to have wing attachment points for 3-inch rockets, bombs or mines and a centreline attachment point for an 18-inch torpedo. It was also to be capable of carrying, beneath each wing, a 90-gallon drop tank to give the aircraft an increased radius of action.

The first of six prototype aircraft, TS371, took off for its maiden test flight on 16 December 1946.

Below: The very first Wyvern, TS371, in bare metallic finish, up on a test flight in 1947; production aircraft would be significantly different in appearance, and in terms of their powerplant. This aircraft crashed later that year, killing its pilot.
Right: VW867, an interim production Wyvern that was retained by the manufacturer during the second half of 1950 for trials work and was the following year also used by Armstrong Siddeley for development work on the Python engine. Significantly different in appearance from the prototype TS371, it nevertheless has the early-production tailplane configuration.

WESTLAND HELICOPTERS

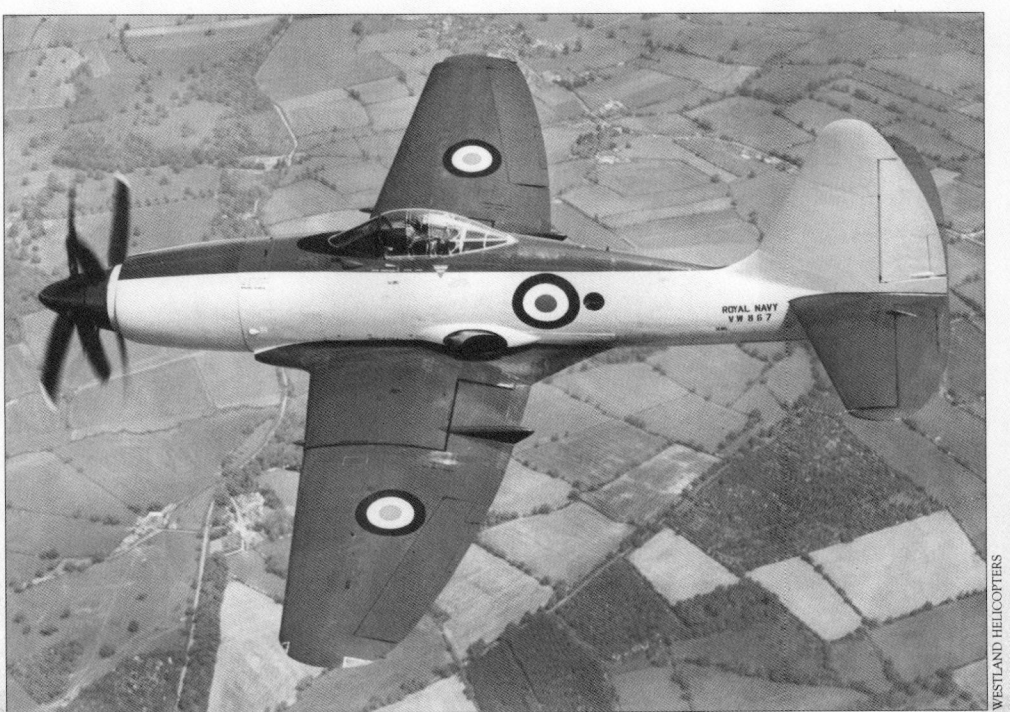

There followed pre-production models known as the Wyvern T.F. Mk 1, all of which were fitted with the Eagle engine. However, Rolls-Royce had so many problems with this powerplant—the last big reciprocating aero-engine to be built by the company—that the delivery of Wyverns to the Royal Navy was had to be delayed until a turbo-prop powerplant became available. Eventually, some 90 aircraft would be built for front-line service. A single two-seat trainer, the Wyvern T. Mk 3, was built, but this variant never entered production, while several other versions were projected but never materialised.

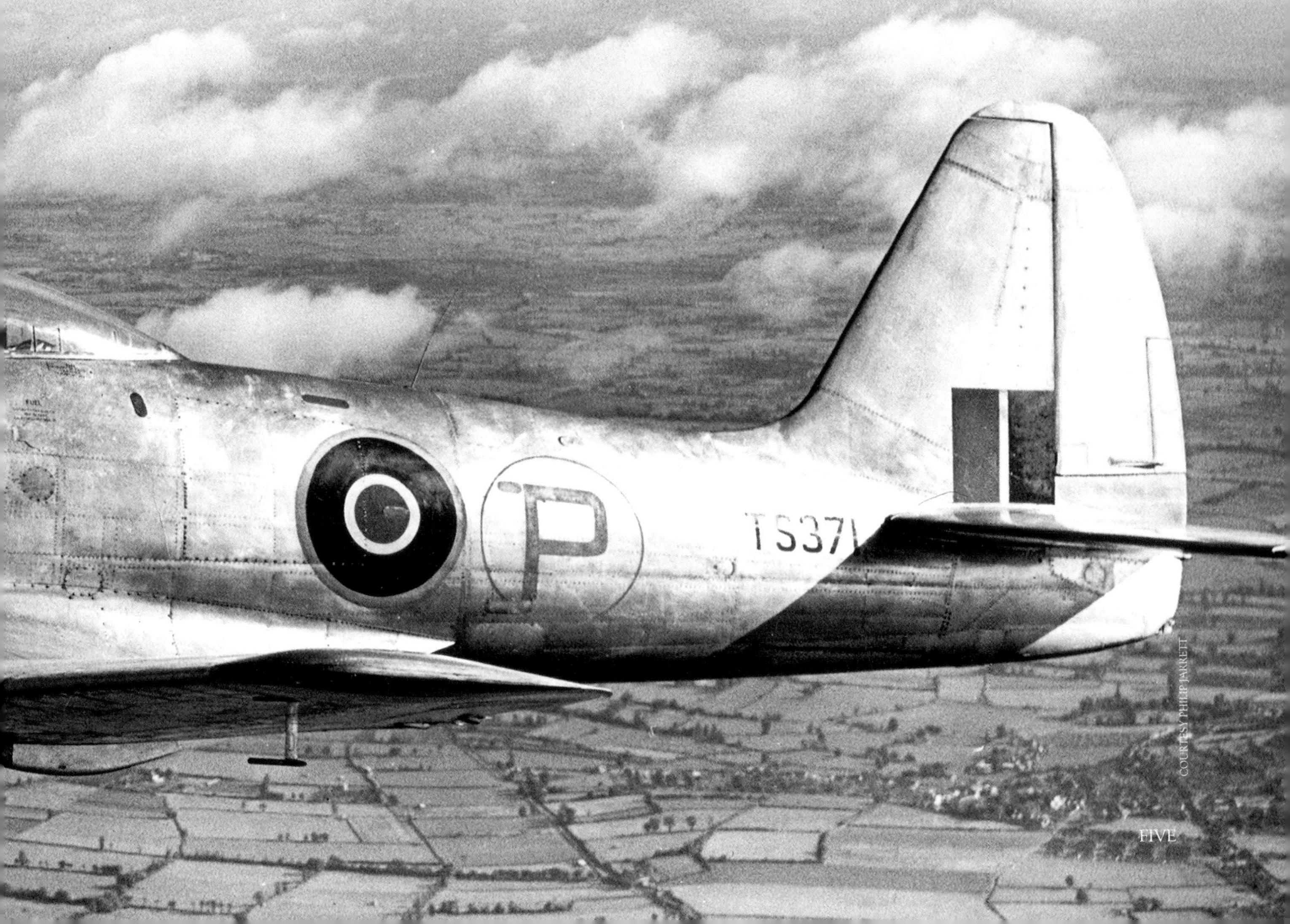

COURTESY PHILIP JARRETT

POWER

THE original Westland W.34 prototype aircraft was powered by the 2,800-cubic-inch Rolls-Royce Eagle piston engine but, owing to numerous problems with that particular powerplant —causing unacceptable delays in its delivery—it was decided to replace it with the Armstrong Siddeley Python turbo-prop; twenty engines were ordered, despite the fact that it had not yet completed its development trials, a decision that would prove to be something of a difficulty throughout the Wyvern's service career in the Fleet Air Arm.

There were at this time two turbo-prop engines undergoing trials within the United Kingdom, one by Rolls-Royce (the Clyde) and the other the Python. RR were not prepared to release their engine until it had completed all its test-bench and in-flight trials, although one example was installed in a flying prototype Wyvern, the T.F. Mk 2, fitted with six-bladed, contra-rotating propellers. However, Armstrong Siddeley were prepared to forego these very important aspects of an aircraft engine's development in order to win the order; and win it they did.

The Python was an unusual turbo-engine in that it was designed with a reversed airflow, that is, air entered the front intake, was reversed through 180 degrees near the rear of the engine and then passed forward through the compressor to drive—initially—a

single-stage turbine; in later models (from the Mk 3 onwards), this mechanism was replaced by dual turbines. The turbine drove a double, four-bladed, 13-foot diameter, contra-rotating propeller which was, at the time, the largest in use on any aircraft in the world.

The engine was designed to run at a constant speed of 7,800rpm. There was only one engine speed control available to the pilot—a single throttle, similar in concept to that used with a pure jet engine. However, when the pilot advanced the throttle, he increased not only the fuel flow but also the pitch angle of the front propeller blades, thereby achieving greater thrust. The pitch of the rear

Opposite, top: The Rolls-Royce Clyde, the unsuccessful contender for the Wyvern contract—and, not entirely incidentally, the world's first twin-spool engine.
Opposite, bottom: Another view of TS371, the Wyvern prototype, showing to advantage the huge contra-rotating propellers for its Rolls-Royce Eagle engine. This powerplant was the last piston aero-engine to be produced by the company.
Above: The second engine to be tried on the Wyvern was the Rolls-Royce Clyde turbo-prop, fitted, uniquely, to VP120, a T.F. Mk 2 (company designation W.35). This aircraft first flew in January 1949, but although the engine showed a good deal of promise its development, like that of the Eagle, was abandoned.
Below: VZ739 was the two-seat trainer version of the aircraft, designated T. Mk 3 (W.38), but this particular variant was not proceeded with. The instructor in the rear seat would have been provided with a periscope.

propeller blades was moved to the same angle of pitch as the front blades by means of a device known as the 'Planet gear system.' The increased propeller pitch increased the load on the engine, which would in normal circumstances decrease in rpm. However, a fuel flow metering control device sensed this change and increased the fuel supply to the engine, thereby maintaining the constant speed at 7,800rpm.

As all fighter pilots know, during in-flight tactics the engine throttle is constantly being changed from high to low or to 'in between' positions, and with a pure jet aircraft the engine does not complain. The Python turbo-prop, however, reacted

Above: Six Eagle-engined Wyverns were built; here one of them reveals its massive powerplant—the largest, as well as the last, piston powerplant built by Rolls-Royce.
Below: VW870, one of the first batch of twenty production-standard Wyvern T.F. Mk 2s, seen here in February 1951. For much of its development the Wyvern served as little more than an engine test-bed, and it is hardly surprising that over six years elapsed between TS371's first flight and the type's official entry into Fleet Air Arm service.

quite differently, and sooner or later the fuel metering control device would 'throw in the towel.' This would lead to a loss of constant speed control, causing fluctuations in engine rpm and jpt (jet pipe temperature). On the other hand, with the aircraft in steady flight—that is, navigating from one point to the next—the engine would purr along for evermore. The engine was originally designed with this characteristic in view, and with the prospect of fitting it to the four-engine Avro Lincoln bomber. In fact, one Lincoln (RF403) had its two outboard nacelles converted to accept Pythons, and with its two inboard Merlins closed down the bomber flew quite happily for hour upon hour on the two turbo-props alone.

The original Python was fitted with only one turbine disc, but, following a pre-take off accident at RNAS Gosport (HMS *St Vincent*) in Hampshire during which the engine turbine spun off the engine shaft and cut through the airframe like a circular saw, it was decided to fit two discs. In one way or another, this reduced the stress on the engine shaft.

If the 'Planet gear system' failed, the rear propeller disc moved automatically to fine pitch, thereby producing a solid 'disc' behind the front propellers and preventing any rearward airflow over the tail of the aircraft. In such an event, the pilot lost effective control of his elevators and rudder and the aircraft would enter a steep descent in a flat attitude and crash. Such mishap could also occur with the Gannet ASW aircraft, which had two turbo-prop engines, one driving each propeller system. If the engine driving the rear set of propellers failed for any reason and the propeller blades reverted to fine pitch

Right: Trainee WRNS mechanics at work on a Wyvern's Python powerplant at Yeovilton, July 1951.

before the pilot could feather them, giving the pilot the same condition as in the Wyvern—a 'disc' which prevented the rearward flow of air over the elevator and rudder—the aircraft would also enter a steep, flat-attitude descent. At least two Gannets were lost in this way, their crews perishing as a result.

During September 1957 the author experienced a 'disc-ing' rear propeller on his Wyvern over a Norwegian fjord, 100 miles north of the Arctic Circle. At the time he had no idea what was happening except that he had noticed silver particles flashing past his cockpit, followed by loss of rudder and

Right: The Python turbo-prop required hefty efflux outlets, and these were situated, port and starboard, above the wing roots. This photograph also shows the style of cockpit canopy fitted to early Wyverns; note also the flat windscreen characteristic of early Wyverns, and the armoured glass behind it, protecting the pilot. The intake alongside the windscreen was to be found slightly higher up the fuselage on production aircraft.

NINE

Top: Westland Wyvern S. Mk 4s in production at Yeovil in 1951. VZ774 is nearest the camera. The folding wing tips were later dispensed with on full-production aircraft, which retained only the main hinges at approximately one-third span.
Above: The Armstrong Siddeley Python production line at Coventry. Armstrong Siddeley's aero engine division was later merged with Bristol Aero Engines to become Bristol Siddeley, which is itself now part of the Roll-Royce organisation.

elevator control and a very high rate of descent. He ejected just in time before the aircraft struck the fjord, his parachute opening almost as he hit the water (see page 27).

When the Wyvern was first deployed to sea, there were several incidents involving loss of power off the catapult. On one occasion an aircraft crashed in front of the carrier *Albion* and the ship passed over it. The pilot, Lieutenant Bruce McFarlane, actually made the first underwater ejection and was picked up astern of the ship by the SAR helicopter. The Wyvern was grounded as a result. Catapult trials were conducted by the Royal Aircraft Establishment at Farnborough, and the engine failed yet again. The ASW Gannet was not experiencing similar failures because its turbo-prop engines were fitted with a recuperator, and with an improved fuel booster pump. The recuperator device was a sphere with a built-in, reversible diaphragm, and was charged with fuel; when high 'g' was applied to it as the aircraft started down the catapult, the diaphragm would reverse, thus supplying the engine with extra fuel, during the time of the aircraft's launch. The engine kept running and the problem was resolved.

ARMSTRONG SIDDELEY PYTHON 3

Axial-flow propeller-turbine engine, 4,100shp plus 1,340lb residual static thrust at sea level. Two 13ft diameter Rotol four-bladed contra-rotating, constant-speed propellers.

Right: The Eagle-engined T.F. Mk 1 VR137 is the only Wyvern now in existence, preserved at the Fleet Air Arm Museum at RNAS Yeovilton—although in fact it never served with an FAA squadron.

Left: An early delivery from Yeovil: VW880, tailhook down, in the care of the Wyvern Receipt and Despatch Unit at RNAS Stretton (HMS *Blackcap*) in early 1953. As related by Commander John Dunphy on page 38, the RDU gave the FAA its first intimate contact with the aircraft and ensured that they were in tip-top condition before being handed over to the squadrons.

Right: VZ761, probably in the spring of 1956 after refurbishment by Westland Aircraft. The 'finlets' added to the Wyvern's tailplane following handling problems are clearly evident, and also—in comparison with VW880 above—this aircraft has the later style of canopy and lacks the AN/APS 13 tail warning radar antenna at the top of the fin. On both aircraft the characteristic F24 camera port on the starboard mid-fuselage is absent.

Although various modifications and improvements were introduced throughout the in-service time of the Python, it remained problematic. The fundamental shortcoming was that the engine was designed for steady, long-haul flights and not for fighter tactics during which a pilot would often demand rapid changes of power output. Unfortunately, in their enthusiasm to keep the military contract going, Armstrong Siddeley never really got to grips with this fact.

Right: A preserved Armstrong-Siddeley Python. The engine was developed from the unsuccessful ASX axial-flow turbojet, and the Wyvern was its sole quantity application.

ELEVEN

FROM THE COCKPIT

THE author flew the Wyvern for the first time on 1 September 1955 at Royal Naval Air Station Ford (HMS *Peregrine*), near Arundel in Sussex. He had requested to fly the aircraft while undergoing his Operational Flying School flight training in the Sea Hawk fighter at RNAS Lossiemouth, and on completion of this flight training he was appointed to the 764 Squadron fighter pilots' 'pool' at RNAS Ford for Wyvern conversion. This Squadron had three Wyvern T.F. Mk 2 aircraft amongst its complement of various aircraft.

It had been decided by Their Lordships at the Admiralty that all Wyvern pilots, prior to going solo, would fly 'back seat' in the Gannet ASW.4, watching the pilot operate the two turbo-prop engines and throttles. I flew with Lieutenant-Commander Stan Farquhar, who would be my Commanding Officer in 831 Squadron—yet to be formed at that time.

The day arrived for my first familiarisation flight in the Wyvern, and my Briefing Officer would be Lieutenant-Commander Gregory. First of all a verbal test was conducted of the Pilot's Notes, aircraft systems and emergency procedures, and then it was out to the aircraft sitting on the flight line to be shown around the machine's exterior, told what to check for and advised of possible external defects. Once this had been done, I climbed up to the cockpit via the step on the port main landing gear oleo. The ejection seat was checked over to ensure that the seat safety pins were in place and that the seat barostat line and drogue 'chute sear were connected to the cockpit rear wall. After climbing into the cockpit and before strapping myself in, Commander Gregory gave me a thorough cockpit brief. I was pleased to discover that the cockpit was considerably larger than that of the Sea Hawk and that of the Vampire FB.5 and 9, and a good deal more comfortable.

The aircraft's engine could be started by either HP (high-pressure) air or a Coffman cartridge. The latter was about four inches in diameter, and when fired it created a huge roar and cloud of black smoke, which almost suffocated the pilot! On this occasion, the engine was started by HP air delivered from a sixteen-cylinder trolley. Throughout the whole of the time that I flew the Wyvern, I only used the cartridge once—when I was diverted to Lossiemouth and there were no HP air bottle trolleys available.

The start-up went smoothly, and on reaching the required rpm for the engine to continue accelerating of its own accord I gave the 'cut off' signal to the ground crew. The propellers at this stage were in fine pitch, and with the propeller 'stop' removed the engine quickly reached 7,800rpm. The wings were spread, and the ground crew checked to ensure that the locks had gone home. All flying controls were checked for full and free movement and the flaps were fully extended, then to be retracted to the take-off position, which was the same as the 'cruise flap' position. The ATC Tower was called for permission to taxi, the wheel chocks were waved away and an airman directed me out of the flight line to the taxi track. The aircraft was easy to taxi thanks to the

TWELVE

COURTESY JOHN DUNPHY

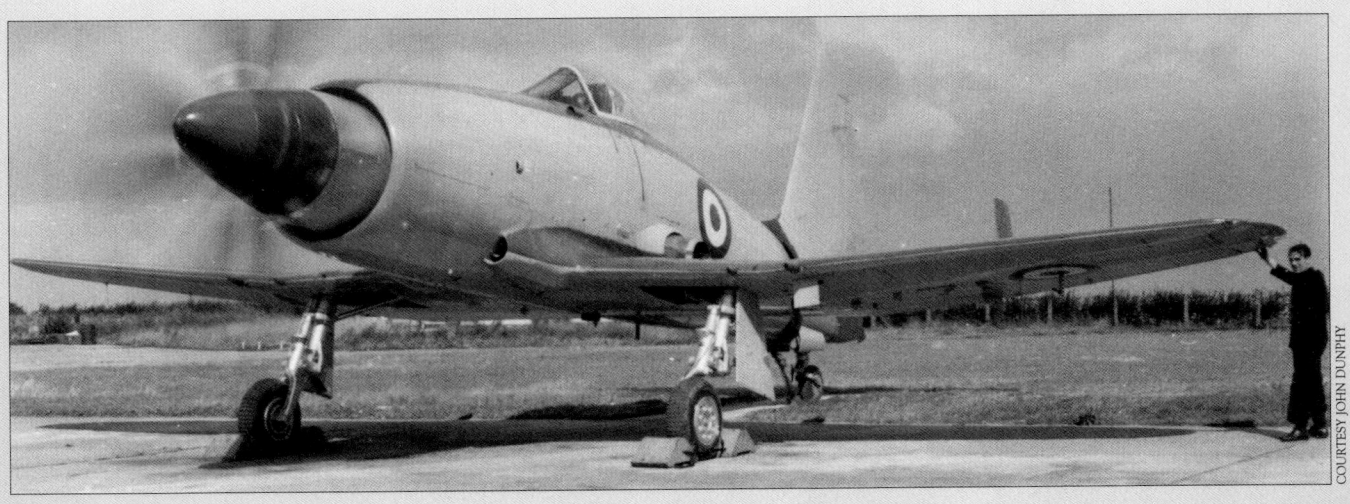

FINAL CHECKS FOR TAKE-OFF

'Promulgated for information and guidance of all concerned by command of Their Lordships,'

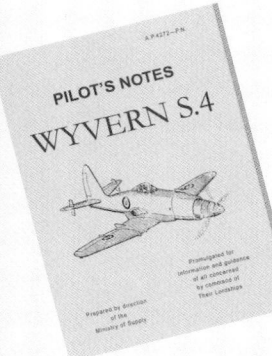

Trimmers	All neutral.
Throttle	Friction tight (catapult only).
Airbrakes	CLOSED.
Fuel	H.P. cock fully ON. Tank selector OUTER WING. Pressure warning light out.
Flaps	TAKE-OFF.
Wings	Spread and locked. Master control lever fully forward. All warning lights and indicators flush with wings. Check full aileron movement.
Instruments	Set. (Inverters ON and indicator black.)
Oxygen	High.
Chartboard	Locked (catapult).
Hood	Locked as required.
Harness	Tight and locked in rear position.
Tailwheel	Locked.

Top: A mid-production Wyvern undergoes ground running tests by the RDU at RNAS Stretton in 1956. The Wyvern's inboard main undercarriage doors typically retracted again once the main gear legs were locked in the 'down' position.
Below: The aircraft's HP air trolleys cleared away (but not yet the chocks), 831 Squadron pilots prepare to taxy out to the main runway at Ford, 1956. A further distinguishing feature of later production Wyverns, as here, was the additional intake on the port fuselage side forward of the windscreen.

AUTHOR'S COLLECTION

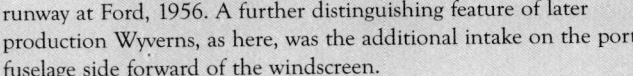

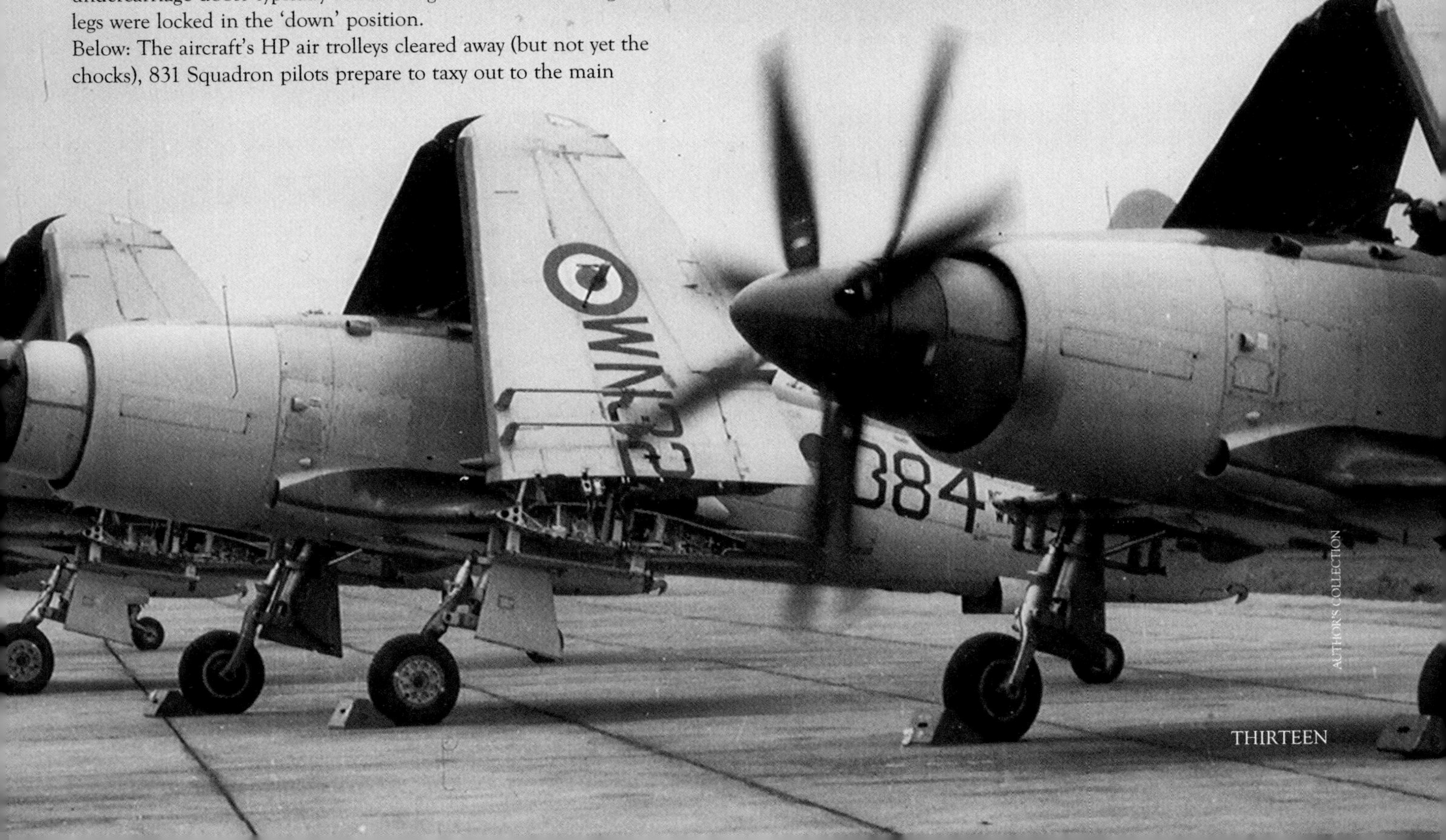

WRITING THE PILOT'S NOTES
Commander R. M. ('Mike') Crosley DSC* RN (RETD)

The 4,100hp axial-flow Python in the Wyvern S.4 ... was started by compressed air. Sixteen eight-foot long compressed-air bottles were loaded on a trolley, a tractor was then engaged to tow it to the aircraft and a twenty-foot hose from four of these bottles was connected to the aircraft's starter turbine. With two men each holding the four chocks in place, and with the pilot having selected 'brakes on' and given the 'thumbs up', the ground crew opened the four valves to a deafening sound of rushing air. The eight-bladed propeller gradually speeded up until the main turbine was doing about 3,500rpm, at which stage the pilot opened the high-pressure fuel cock and the main jets ignited—with a long flame appearing from the jet pipe and a noise like a dozen elephants trumpeting denoting success.

If a full-power engine run was required with the Wyvern, the aircraft had to be tied down to ring bolts in a concrete blast pen, otherwise the ground crew holding the chocks in place could become airborne and tend to disappear over the far hedge. This sort of thing actually happened on board *Albion* when Wyverns of 813 Squadron were returning to Portsmouth from Malta ...

I found that take-off was smooth and all three flying controls responded well with small movements and light stick forces. The aircraft flew off the ground at about 120 knots and once the flaps and wheels were up it accelerated quickly to 200 knots, its best climbing speed. Ten thousand feet was reached in 2½ minutes at the light load at which I was flying. I throttled back to carry out some stalls, flaps up, flaps at 'max lift' for take-off, flaps fully down, power on, power at 'flight-idle', wheels up and wheels down. Then, at 15,000 feet I did a few steep turns at full throttle until stalling incidence was reached, managing to pull a steady 4g without having to reduce height or speed below about 180 knots throughout. This minimum turning circle would have been nearly twice the radius of a Seafire 47 or Sea Fury, and the Wyvern would have presented both of them and many other fighters with a sitting target.

The Wyvern was a classic example of how it is impossible to 'get something for nothing' in a 'multi-role' aircraft. It could lift only 30 per cent more bombs than a Fury and go only 50 miles further towards its target with them. Yet, unlike the Sea Fury, it could not take on the mantle of a fighter once it had dropped its load, for its power/weight ratio was half, and its wing-loading double that of a Sea Fury in a similar condition.

Its ceiling at a weight of 24,000lb was 25,000 feet and the extra drag of a steep turn—an essential manœuvre to try to avoid enemy fighters in a dogfight—would immediately slow it down to the stall, requiring a large loss in height to retain flying speed. However, sea-level fuel consumption trials at Manby showed that the Python prop-jet combination was economical in miles per gallon at low altitudes compared with a pure jet of the same weight, so that the Wyvern's radius of action over the sea under the enemy's radar—about 400 miles—would be more acceptable.

In fact the Wyvern's sea-level approach pattern completely baffled the Navy's radar defence arrangements in the absence of AEW Skyraider support for, when we flew it in 813 Squadron in the Mediterranean the following year, we always managed to get into rocket-firing range of HM ships before a single gun had been turned in our direction. Even if they had seen us coming, their larger AA guns could only be traversed at the speed of a Swordfish and would have been ineffective in any case ...

The Wyvern's approach and landing was as easy as the take-off. It had a good forward view, with the nose acting as a perfect incidence indicator needing only an occasional glance at the airspeed indicator to check the airspeed on the deck approach. With a long tailwheel strut and a long-stroke 'trailing link' undercarriage shock absorber system, the Wyvern sat down and stayed down on the deck in all touch-downs not above a vertical velocity of 14ft/sec. Above this the undercarriage would fail, the metal prop would strike the deck and slivers of steel would fly everywhere. Following the death of one of the flight deck party during deck trials, an Admiralty Fleet Order was issued forbidding anyone to be near the Wyvern during deck landings. This included the usual crowd of aviators watching from 'Goofers' Gallery' on the island—300 feet away!

The relative touch-down speed of about 80 knots was nearly twice as fast as that of the Seafire, so that controllability and fast reactions from the pilot to advice from Nick Goodhart's 'magical mirror' were essential. But speed control was easy to maintain throughout the entire approach with very small throttle movements, the contra-prop, powerful rudder and lockable tailwheel ensuring straight landings and take-offs, even when taking off from airfields in strong cross winds. ...

When checking the Wyvern's maximum indicated airspeed, I found that at all the weights that I flew it, it only managed about 300 knots at maximum power at sea level when carrying wing stores, not the 345 knots at sea level stated by the makers. This was a bit too slow to loop and roll off the top after lobbing a bomb or rocket—the normal method adopted in the LABS (Low-Altitude Bombing System)—so the Wyvern had to break away by steep turning.

Even at 300 knots' indicated airspeed the Wyvern's high wing loading (its 70lb/sq ft being double that of the Seafire 47) limited its turning ability to a huge radius at no more than four sustainable g, making it an easy target for computed, light AA fire should it ever get near enough to a Russian ship to release its weapon; neither would it stand much chance in a dogfight against any fighter, piston or jet.

About twenty hours' flying was needed to gain enough experience of the Wyvern to write Pilot's Notes. Having only simple navigation devices and needing no observer to accompany the pilot to operate the ever more complicated electronics about to be fitted to the Scimitar and Sea Vixen, the Wyvern was extraordinarily easy to write about. The usual flights were made to check miles/gallon, lateral control with bomb hang-ups, night landings and control in the dive up to about 560 knots indicated and up to 0.76 Mach, at which speed the prop tips were supersonic and people in the Lincolnshire pubs wanted to know what all the noise was about!

FROM THE COCKPIT

Above: Commander R. M. Crosley at the controls of Wyvern S. Mk 4. As a Lieutenant-Commander, 'Mike' Crosley assumed command of the Wyvern-equipped 813 Squadron in late 1954; he had earlier written the Pilot's Notes for the type.
Below: Lieutenant Mike Doust lands a Wyvern S. Mk 4 at Ford.

fuel to reach the engine in order to maintain a constant rpm. The acceleration down the runway was extremely high, and smooth—far better than that experienced in the Sea Hawk. There was no need to raise the tail: the Wyvern lifted off comfortably in a three-point attitude at about 102 knots.

Once airborne, I retracted the undercarriage and flaps, ensuring that the engine 'Stop' was in once the gear was up, and climbed away at the recommended indicated airspeed of 165 knots. Once clear of the airfield circuit I switched to the approach radio channel, all the while climbing to 20,000 feet and keeping an eye open for other aircraft—especially civil airliners which flew into Gatwick and London Airports. Apart from Ford Air Station itself, there were RAF Tangmere and Thorney Island to the west, RAE Farnborough to the north and Shoreham civil airport to the east. The local airspace was therefore

movable tail wheel, and because one also sat fairly high on the ejection seat there was a reasonable view over the engine cowling and nose of the aircraft.

I stopped just short of the duty runway, carried out the final take-off checks and called the Tower for permission to line up and take off. I taxied forward slightly on the runway to straighten the tail wheel, then locked it for take-off, and opened up the engine to full power (that is, full propeller pitch). There was no increase in rpm although the jpt of course rose. As the throttle was fully opened, the propeller pitch was coarsened off, at the same time allowing more

very congested. (It was mainly for this reason that the Navy finally closed Ford in the 1960s—after continual use since World War I—and concentrated its fighter bases at Yeovilton and Lossiemouth.)

Incidentally, as soon as a novice Wyvern pilot taxied, the Briefing Officer always made his way to the ATC Tower, just in case the airman experienced a problem, had an emergency or required advice. He would always be in the Tower for the first three to five familiarisation flights.

At this point it is worth mentioning why the engine 'Stop' was so important As previously

GETTING TO GRIPS

The Author

The Wyvern's cockpit was very large in comparison with those of naval fighters of the day; in terms of roominess, it was on a par with that of the F-4K Phantom. The standard six flight instruments—A/H, ASI, altimeter, compass, VSI and T/S—were grouped together in one panel immediately in front of the pilot's control stick. To the right of the main panel were located the engine instruments, comprising the rpm, jpt and oil pressure gauges, together with the fuel gauges. To the left were the Machmeter, radio altimeter and various selectors including those for RATOG (rocket-assisted take-off gear) and cartridge starting.

The aircraft was fitted with a standard gyro gun sight (the Mk 4E), mounted above the main instrument panel. It was well sited and did not interfere with the pilot's view out of the cockpit. Immediately below the GGS was the pilot's plotting table, which could be slid out or retracted according to requirements. The radio altimeter limit lights were just to the right of the gyro gun sight and slightly below the cockpit coaming.

The cockpit canopy was of two designs, the TF.2 and early S.4s having an all-Perspex model, with reinforcing strips (also of Perspex) around the interior surfaces towards the rear, and the later S.4s having an 'all-clear' model with a metal cap at the rear. The S.4's windshield was flat rather than curved. The Martin-Baker Mk 2B ejection seat (Mk 1B in some aircraft) was quite capable of punching through either canopy with no detrimental effect upon the seat or its automatic systems. The front of the seat was fitted with a 'pee tube' so that the pilot could if need be relieve himself during a long flight.

All in all the Wyvern had a very good pilot's cockpit. Everything was readily to hand, and the visibility to the front and sides was excellent. The author thoroughly enjoyed flying and operating the aircraft!

Right: Plugging the air feed starter hose into a Wyvern. The aircraft here is temporarily assigned to the Royal Navy Handling Section, under the auspices of No 4 Squadron RAF at Manby, for the purpose of compiling the Pilots' Notes—the 'handbook', as it were, for aircrews. The photograph clearly shows the laborious climb to the cockpit facing the Wyvern pilot—albeit aided by a footstep incorporated into the main gear leg and two further steps recessed into the port fuselage (the latter highlighted by near-vertical, thin black stripes).

mentioned, the Python was a constant-speeding turbo-prop engine, and thrust was adjusted by changing the pitch of the propellers. If the propellers were fined off to about 19 degrees, the 'Stop' would prevent any further reduction in pitch, and then the engine rpm would start to decrease and the jpt would increase, resulting in a possible engine failure. If a pilot were going to slow-fly, then he switched the engine 'Stop' switch to 'Out' and the engine would continue constant-speeding. When flying with the undercarriage down, the 'Stop' was automatically disengaged by the lowering of the landing gear; however, to make certain the pilot always manually selected it 'Out'.

At 20,000 feet I accelerated to 250 knots and carried out general handling, making dummy circuits and approaches. Aerobatics were not permitted in the aircraft, except for a barrel roll provided positive 'g' were maintained In bad weather or at night the Wyvern proved to be a steady aircraft: it stayed where it was pointed, and on bad-weather approaches and in poor visibility it would remain steady, a characteristic that could be attributed to its heaviness, its high wing loading and the Youngman flaps which allowed the aircraft to fly at a steady 120 knots almost to touch-down. Circuits and landings were generally easy to fly, the actual size of the circuit being much the same as that for a small jet, although the final approach was a little longer with a good straightaway. The flaps were huge when compared with those of other aircraft, and enabled the pilot to fly more slowly—especially useful when flying from a carrier. It was not necessary to execute a 'flare out', only to fly down to about 102 knots, whereupon the aircraft would touch down in a perfect three-point attitude. If flapless approach and landing were made, then one would 'wheel' the aircraft on with the tail slightly high.

The Wyvern was easy to handle—if perhaps a little slow to respond to changes in roll, pitch and yaw at

Right: The author starting up his aircraft at RNAS Lossiemouth prior to making a live bombing run on Garvie Island, 1956. The ground crewmen are in the process of disconnecting the HP air supply hose.

COURTESY PHILIP JARRETT

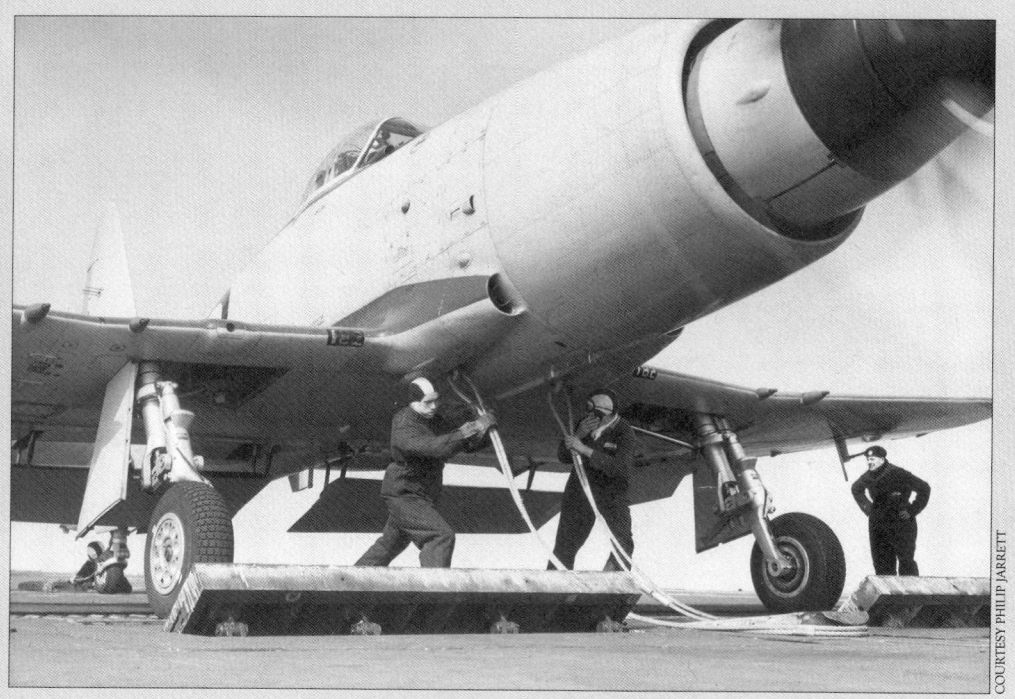

Left: Flight-deck crewmen attach the catapult strop to an 813 Squadron Wyvern preparatory to launching the aircraft, 1955. Along the leading edge of the starboard can be seen (left to right) the faired muzzles of the two starboard 20mm cannon; the aperture for the G45 cine camera (which operated automatically, provided the master switch was 'On', whenever the guns or underwing rocket projectiles were fired); and the three numerals of aircraft's call-sign
Below: A Wyvern caught at the moment of departure from one of HMS *Eagle*'s catapults. The strop can be seen falling away.

that speed—and it felt comfortable. It was possible to fly with the canopy open. In the course of one flight by the author, the canopy locking mechanism failed and the canopy closed suddenly, knocking his 'bone dome' over his eyes. Nevertheless, a safe landing was executed!

Carrier launches and recoveries required concentration. The carrier circuit was usually joined at 400 feet and 250 knots, the pilot flying upwind for about half to three-quarters of mile before he broke left downwind. By the time he was straight and level downwind, the carrier was abeam to port; and then

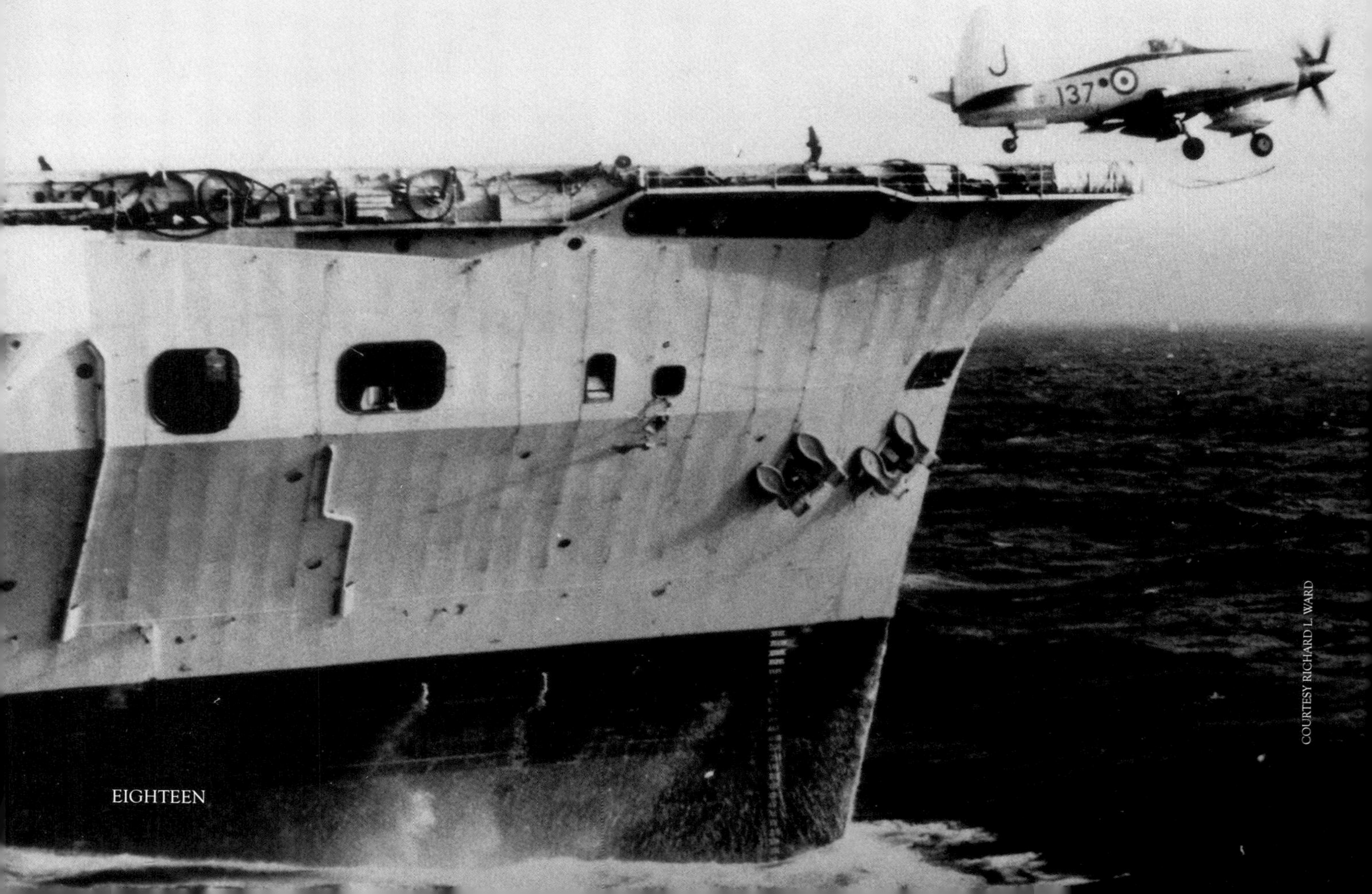

COURTESY RICHARD L WARD

the left turn on to finals was commenced, landing gear, full flap and tailhook having been lowered. Height was maintained as the approach was made to finals, and about half way round the deck-landing sight would be picked up. Power was then reduced in order to start the descent to the carrier deck, the pilot holding the aircraft in a nose-high attitude so that the airspeed fell off to about 102 knots, the touch down speed for the average landing weight— and the speed at which the flight attitude would be 'three-point'.

As the approach was made, the mirror deck landing sight's central source light was kept in line with the green horizontal bars either side of it; if the aircraft went high the source light would stay at amber and if low it would change to red. If the Landing Safety Officer (LSO) was unhappy with the approach, he would flash red lights at the pilot from the top of the sight, indicating that he wanted him to 'wave off' and attempt another approach. The angled flight deck on the major fleet carriers was about 350 feet long, with a wide white centre line from the round down, and four arrester wires were rigged at the beginning of the landing deck, the mirror sight being set for the aircraft to catch No. 2 wire. However, even if the aircraft caught No. 4 wire, there was still plenty of deck left to pull out on.

As soon as the Wyvern came to a stop, the pilot throttled back to idling and the aircraft would automatically roll backwards (owing to the tension on the arrester wire) and the deck-landing hook would disengage. A flight-deck airman handler would rush over indicating that it was safe for the pilot to raise the hook, start taxying forward, fold the wings and raise the flaps. He would then pass the aircraft on to the next handler, who would direct the pilot into the forward aircraft park at the starboard bow. Once the wheel chocks and parking

Right, upper: Its flaps lowered for take-off, 827 Squadron's WL880 is prepared for launch aboard *Eagle*. The hold-back gear attached to the tailwheel leg is in position.

Right, lower: A Wyvern roars away from *Eagle* during the type's early flight-deck trials. In later years on board carriers, catapult strops would be snared by a 'bridle catcher' projecting from the flight deck-edge as the aircraft departed, facilitating their re-use.

chains had been clipped on to the aircraft, thus ensuring that it was secured to the deck, the pilot would be given the signal to cut his engine and climb out—after the ejection seat safety pins had been inserted in order to render the seat safe.

Throughout the summer months over British waters—and over the Mediterranean—the Wyvern pilot normally wore a grey lightweight flight suit, or coverall. However, at nights and over northern waters he would wear his immersion flight suit, which protected him against the cold-water temperatures. The author was very glad that he was wearing his immersion suit when he ejected from his Wyvern and landed in Harstadtfjord, a hundred miles north of the Arctic Circle. Boy, was the water cold! In addition to flight overalls, Wyvern pilots also wore a cooling suit when flying over the Mediterranean. This was a nylon type body suit with small air pipes woven into it: air from the engine compressor blew over the pilot's body, and in doing so would evaporate any sweat and thereby cool him. Although 'g' leggings had been introduced to FAA service, Wyvern pilots did not wear them.

During 1957, 831 Squadron began to encounter deck-landing problems. The first occurrence was off Scotland one morning, when one of the pilots experienced an arrester-wire failure. With everybody screaming at him over the radio 'Brakes, brakes, brakes!' he came to a halt a few feet from the end of the flight deck, almost standing on his nose! His arrester hook had sliced right through the wire, and

Above: Lieutenants John Webster (left) and Peter McKern of 830 Squadron demonstrating the attire of the well-dressed Wyvern pilot. This photograph was taken in late 1956, at the time of the Suez Crisis: the .38 revolvers were not peacetime issue!
Below: A Wyvern pilot's view of his carrier (in this instance *Ark Royal*) immediately before touch-down. A flight deck as empty as this would be a very unlikely luxury, although the angled deck seen here provided him at least with an unobstructed landing strip.

FROM THE COCKPIT

LEVEL YOUR WINGS AND CUT

Vice-Admiral Sir Roy Halliday KBE DSC

I took command of 813 Naval Air Squadron in November 1956 at RNAS Ford, having familiarised on the Wyvern in 764 Squadron for about a month, also at Ford. My first solo on type was on 23 July 1956, and I recall being somewhat alarmed at the time by the sheer size of the aircraft as compared with the average single-seat naval aircraft of the day. The Wyvern was ponderous both in the air and on the ground, but to the pilot it had the feeling of reliability and ruggedness when he was strapped in the fairly confined cockpit.

It was not an aerobatic aircraft, and although some foolhardy types did try to disprove this (with no great success), its manœuvrability as a torpedo attack aircraft and a glide bomber was adequate. Most of our work-up ashore was concentrated on these two roles.

Its limitation was as a deck-landing aircraft—a disadvantage for an aircraft intended for embarked operations. With its unusually long nose from cockpit to propeller (some thirteen feet, I recall) and with the aircraft in a three-point attitude for landing (some 10 knots above stall with flaps down), the visibility ahead with wings level was non-existent. This meant that one's approach to the round-down was a continuous left-hand turn in order to see the batsman (there was no mirror sight in those days). His final signal was inevitably 'Level your wings and cut' as one crossed the round-down. This last movement was dangerous because the Wyvern's aileron response at low speed was very poor and usually needed the assistance of discreetly applied starboard rudder to effect the levelling of the aircraft before engaging a wire.

The problem of deck-landing tended initially to be uppermost in squadron pilots' minds. As they gained confidence in the aircraft, most of them got over the problem, but unfortunately some otherwise competent pilots were unhappy and this wastage rate of otherwise good aircrew was unacceptable.

The Wyvern was in my opinion poorly designed for carrier operations, but fortunately since then, with the advent of aircraft with excellent forward vision coupled with the angled deck, the problem no longer exists.

In summary, the Wyvern did not have a full opportunity to demonstrate its operational capabilities—the potential was there. Its time in front-line service was comparatively short.

Below: A Westland Wyvern of 813 NAS (left) on board *Eagle* during Vice-Admiral 'Gus' Halliday's period in command of the Squadron. The view forward out of the cockpit with the aircraft in a three-point attitude—referred to above—may be compared with that from the cockpit of the contemporary Hawker Sea Hawk fighter (right).

COURTESY RICHARD L. WARD

COURTESY RICHARD L. WARD

COURTESY PHILIP JARRETT

COURTESY RICHARD L. WARD

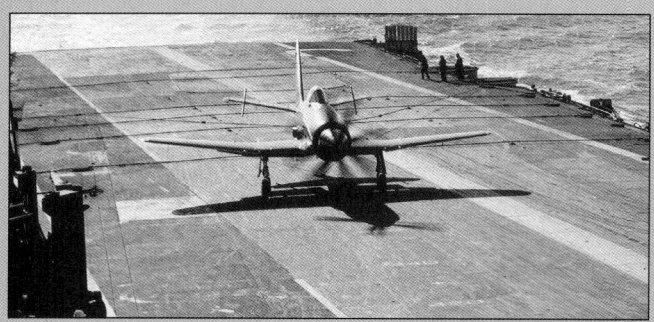

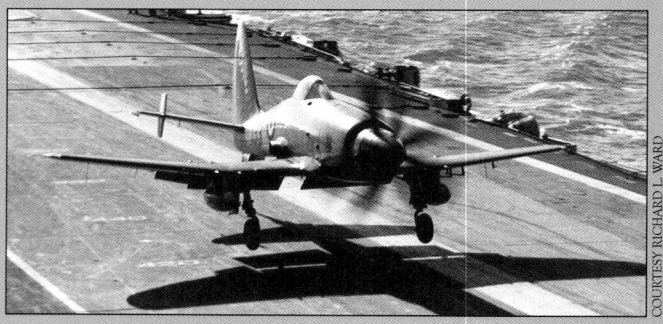

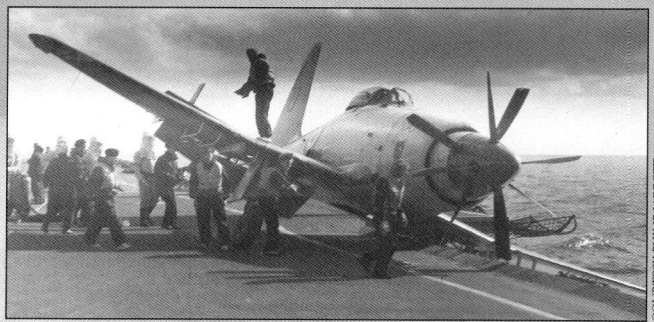

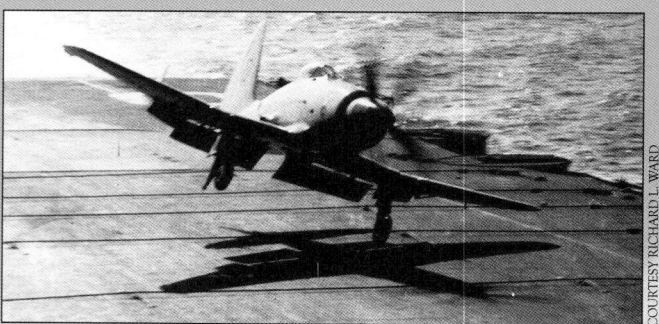

Above: How not to land a Wyvern at sea: (clockwise from top left) a pre-production aircraft during trials, a bit adrift but safely 'hooked'; an 827 NAS aircraft performing a 'bolter', the pilot missing the wires—deliberately or otherwise—and about to 'go round' for another attempt; not the best landing ever seen by an 831 NAS pilot; and a rather expensive touch-down, again by 831 Squadron.

had missed the next couple of wires, before he came to a screeching halt. What had happened?

The 'bill' of the Wyvern's arrester hook looked very much like a firmer chisel from side on, whereas other naval aircraft hooks were rounded. *Ark Royal*'s arrester system had been upgraded to take heavier aircraft, and therefore had wires of a greater diameter, thereby presenting a larger surface area to the aircraft's hook. Consequently, either the hook picked up the wire properly or its sharp 'front end' sliced into the wire and a combination of the aircraft's weight and speed caused the wire to fail. The Wyvern was banned from further deck-landing until the problem could be resolved.

Ashore at RNAS Ford, and at RAE Farnborough, trials were carried out with a redesigned hook,

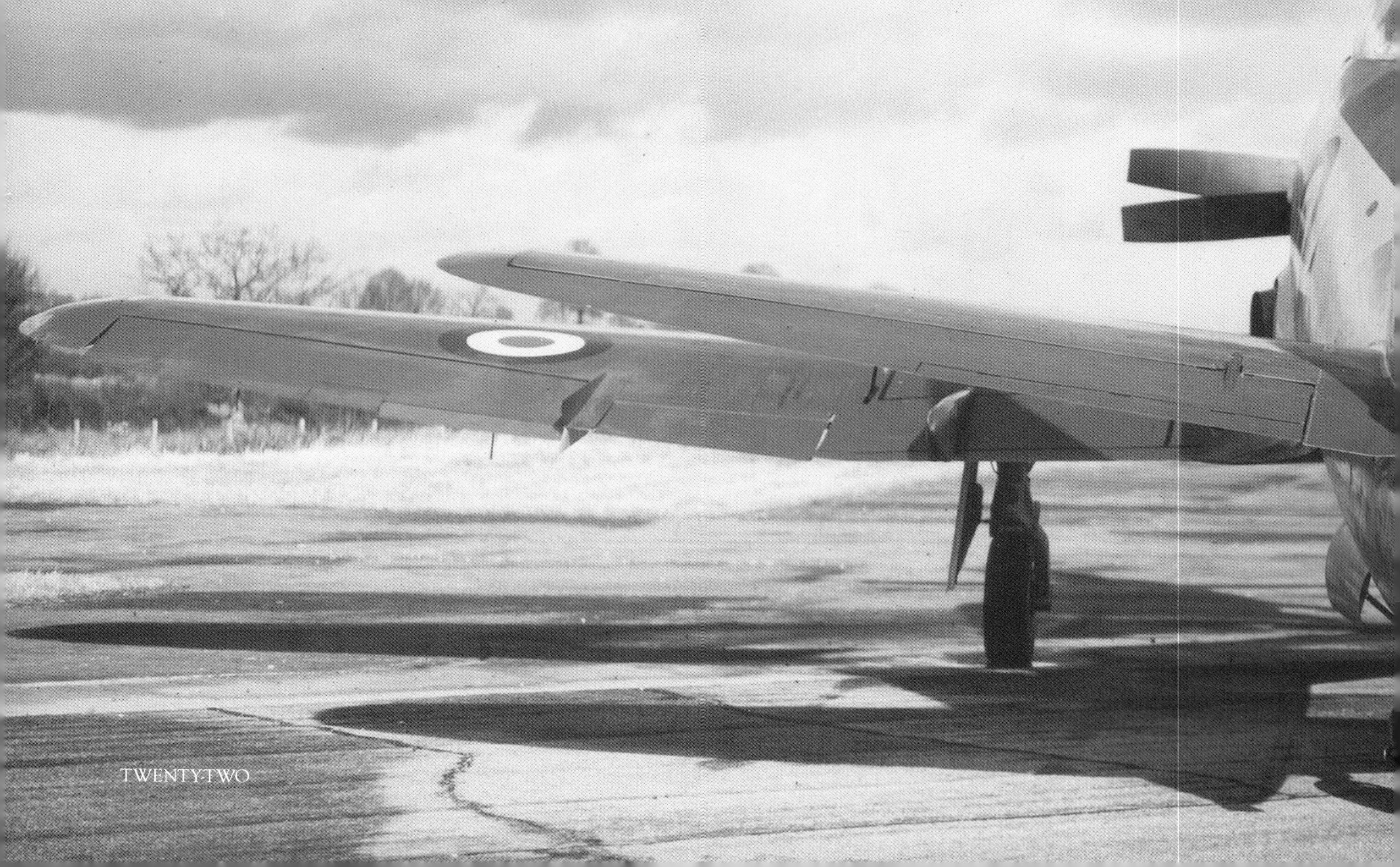

COURTESY JOHN DUNPHY

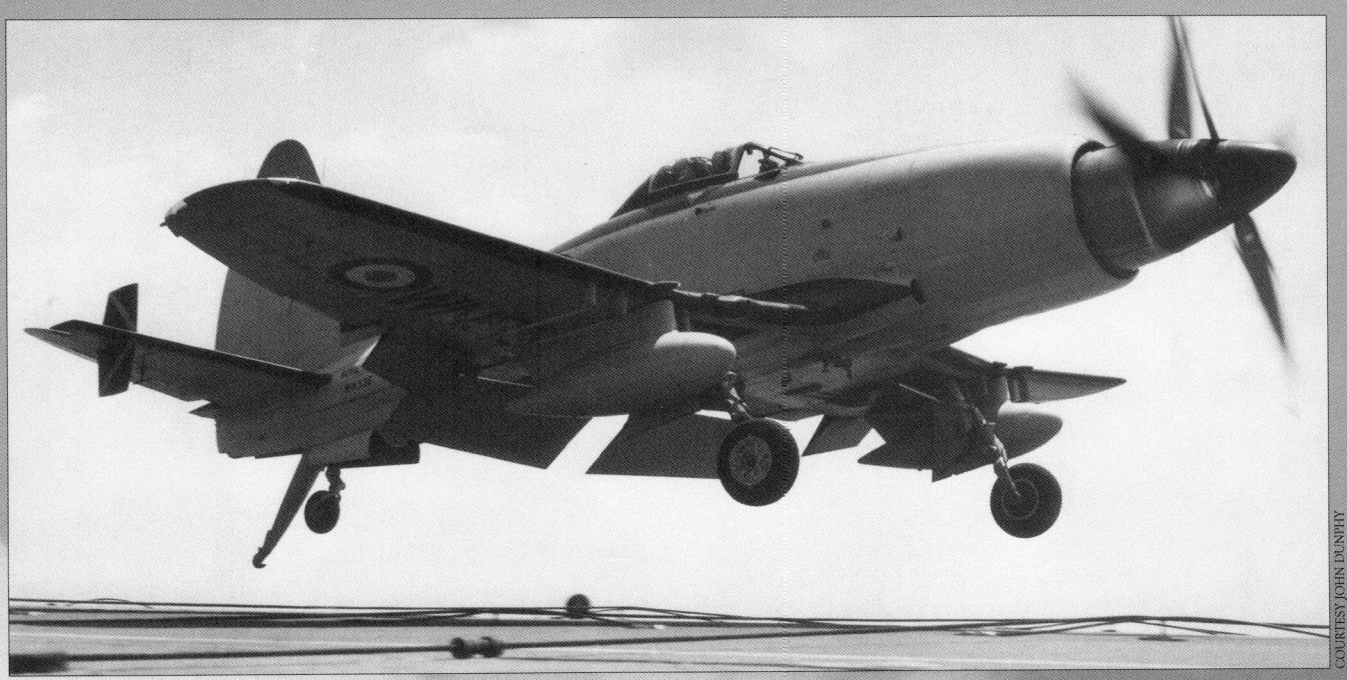

featuring a bill and throat of increased curvature. Numerous trials were carried out and the problem was eventually resolved, and so 831 Squadron re-embarked aboard *Ark Royal.*

This unit's final disembarkation was carried out whilst the carrier was tied up to a buoy in the Firth of Forth, just below the Forth Bridge. Some aircraft went to Lossiemouth and the others flew south to Ford, where they would be handed over to the re-forming 813 Squadron. Although the aircraft would remain in service for another two years with 813 Squadron, it was a very sad day when the 831 Wyvern days came to an end. 831 would not disappear altogether: it would be resurrected as the RN's Air Electronics Squadron, taking over from 751 Squadron at RNAS Culdrose and equipped with Gannet A.S.W. Mk 4 aircraft.

Above: A textbook three-point landing by WN336 of 830 Squadron, late 1956. This particular Wyvern would look rather less smart before long—see page 67.
Below: VW870, a Mk 2 converted to Mk 4 standard, though still lacking the tailplane 'finlets', early 1951

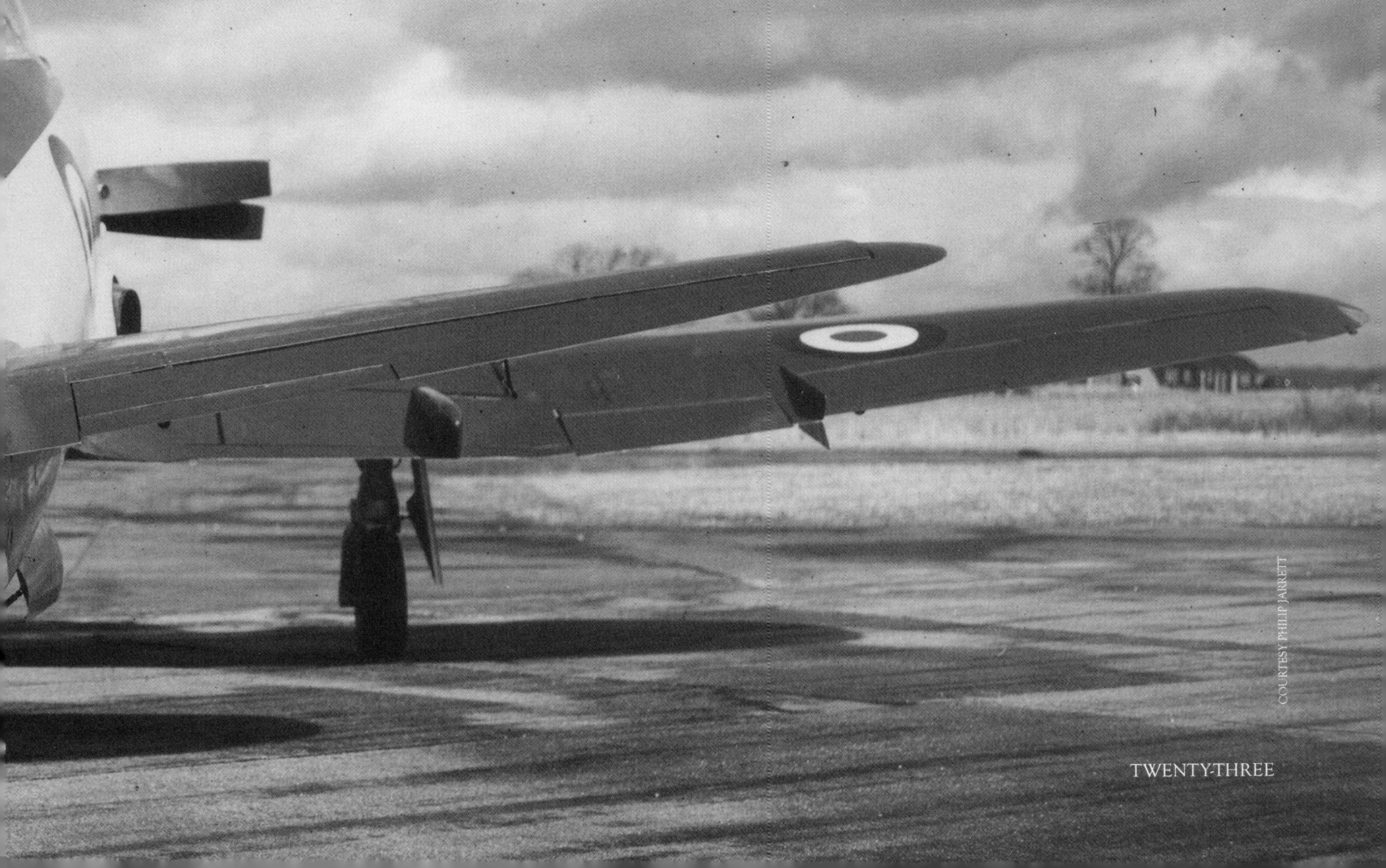

COURTESY PHILIP JARRETT

SPIRAL DIVES versus SPINS

Lieutenant-Commander (AE) (P) John Norman RN (RETD)

I was probably the least successful Wyvern pilot, quite undeserving of the respect in which we are held! During my time with 813 Squadron, some of my deck-landing problems undoubtedly lay in the briefing that the approach speed was to be at about 98 knots because of the limitations of the arrester gear, rather than the 100–102 knots that Mike Crosley quotes in his book.* This made a world of difference, especially when passing through the ship's funnel fumes on the way to the angled deck.

I managed to spin my trusty steed when practising low flying with wheels and flaps down. Without warning, the left wing dropped and she fell out of my hands. Recovery by the usual method took 4,500 feet or so; luckily, I had started my efforts at 8,000. Wildly excited, after a cup of what passed for coffee in those days, I reported to my fellow pilots, triggering a hot debate about spiral dives *versus* spins. I stood out for spins, and had an amicable chat with the Boss. 'What height did you start at?' 'Eight thousand feet, sir.' He looked me straight in the eye. 'Compressibility!' he said.

Morris Hedges was a master of the Wyvern. I remember a beautiful evening display at Hal Far that was fully up to anyone's standards—Sea Hawk jockeys included.

In 1957, as MTP (Maintenance Test Pilot) at Fleetlands, I tested the first few overhauled Wyverns, starting with VZ772, which went to Ford. Jock Tofts was SP (Senior Pilot) of the Squadron and seemed quite pleased with our product, but told me that they had tweaked the top temperature a bit.

During type conversion with 827 Squadron, I managed to leave a wet runway on landing at Ford by closing the throttle too soon, cutting off the airflow over the rudder. The braked wheels having aquaplaned, I careered across the grass until the wheels sank in, tipping the aircraft on to its nose, whereupon the props went all agricultural—with a most satisfactory noise and clods of earth everywhere. That taught me to sit her firmly down, and do nothing more until a good, steady roll-out had been established.

Within its limitations, the Wyvern was a comfortable aircraft to fly, steady in the dive, just able to outrun a Sea Fury at low level, utterly unable to mix it with the Sea Hawk and not worth the lives lost in the development and operation of its Python engine. I think we should have bought the Skyraider, the airborne early warning version of which served so well and for so long.

A passing thought: where is 813's line book, beautifully put together, with comments on the Wyvern and on the Squadron's previous freak, the Firebrand?

* Commander R. M. 'Mike' Crosley DSC* RN, *Up in Harm's Way: Flying with the Fleet Air Arm*, Pen & Sword Aviation (Barnsley, 2005).

Below: 813 Squadron Wyverns airborne from RNAS Ford. 813 was the first front-line Wyvern unit to be commissioned, on 20 May 1953.

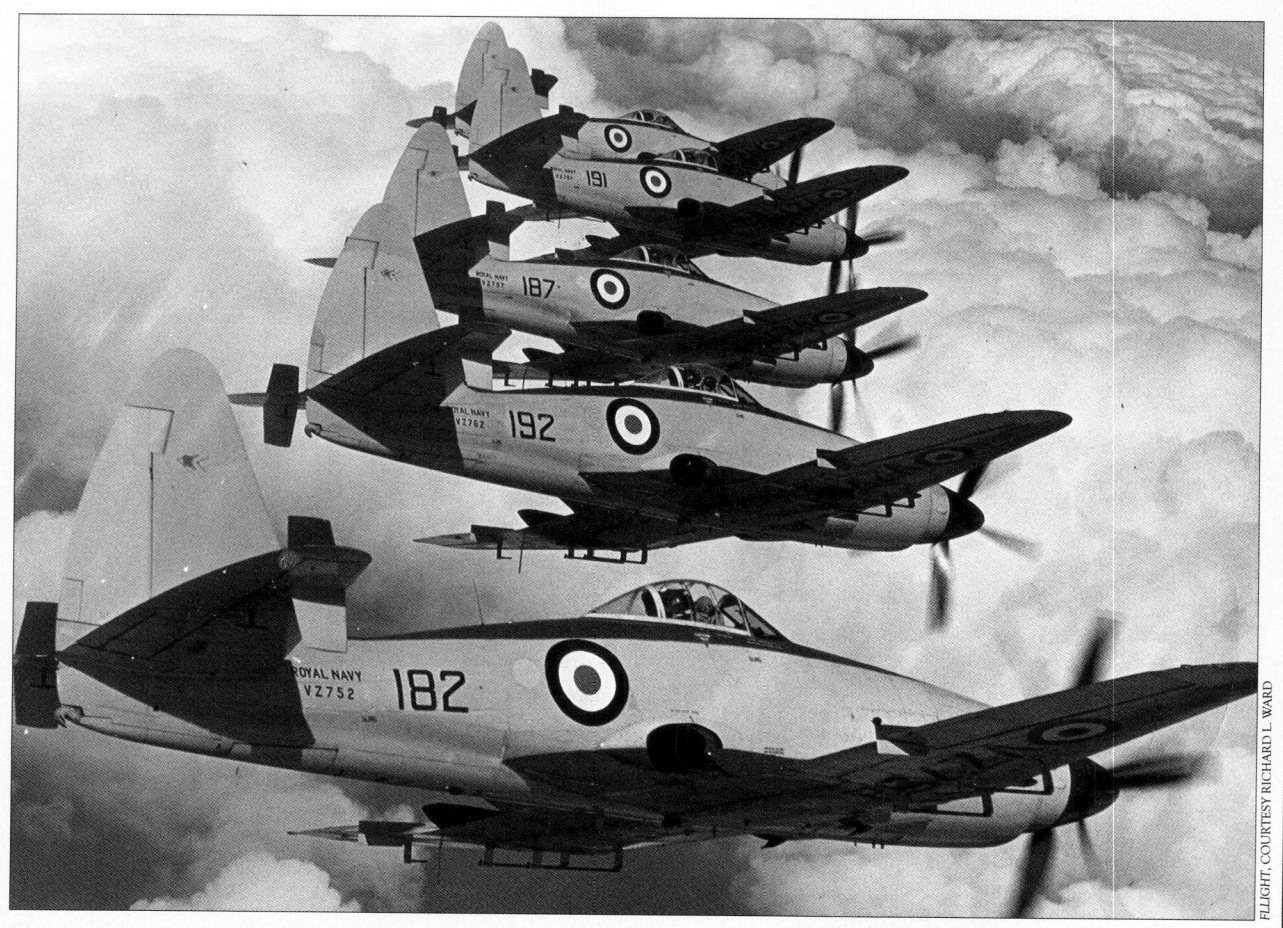

FROM THE COCKPIT

Above: 813 Naval Air Squadron Wyvern S. Mk 4s up from Ford for a publicity sortie in 1954 and maintaining immaculate formation. The aircraft have the early 'ribbed' cockpit canopy.

Below: A late-production Wyvern S.4 of 831 NAS, photographed in 1956 or 1957 from beneath another aircraft of the same unit. The tail code letter indicates assignment to the fleet carrier *Ark Royal*.

TWENTY-FIVE

WYVERN

TIME TO GO

'Promulgated for information and guidance of all concerned by command of Their Lordships'

Ejection seat Mk 1B or 2B

WARNING—The pilot must ensure that the safety pin is removed and stowed before flight and must lock the handle against the possibility of accidental withdrawal on the ground before leaving the cockpit. All personnel must ensure that the firing handle is locked (i.e., fabric safety strap passed through handle and secured by its safety pin) before entering the cockpit.

(i) Either a Mk 1B or Mk 2B pilot ejection seat may be fitted [to the Wyvern]. Both seats incorporate a type ZD harness, a container to support the weight of the Mk 3A (1B seat) or Mk 8A (2B seat) back-type parachute and a seat well in which is carried the K dinghy pack type J and emergency oxygen supply. On both seats the harness release lever is on the outboard side of the starboard thigh guard and the seat adjustment lever . . . is on the starboard side of the seat.

(ii) No automatic separation facilities are available on the Mk IB seat; the pilot must manually release himself from the seat after ejection.

(iii) The Mk 2B seat is fitted with fully automatic facilities which, after ejection, separate the pilot from the seat and open his parachute. After ejection, at heights of 10,000ft and below, a barostat causes the automatic cycle to commence; after 5 seconds, or 3 seconds when Martin-Baker Mod. 204 is embodied, the seat harness is released, as are the face screen, firing handle and headrest pad. An apron attached to the seat then pitches the pilot head first out of the seat, at the same time opening his parachute.

(iv) A 60ft/sec ejection gun is fitted. When Mod. 573 and Martin-Baker Mod. 285 are embodied, this gun is replaced by an 80ft/sec gun. It is essential that the pilot is aware of the Mod. stage of his seat, since the type of gun fitted affects the minimum safe ejection height . . .

(v) A manual override D-ring is fitted over the ripcord D-ring and, when pulled, disconnects the parachute from the seat. In this event it is subsequently necessary to release the seat harness and pull the ripcord D-ring.'

Abandoning:
1. Reduce speed.
2. Jettison hood.
3. Retract GGS [gyro gun sight].
4. Parachute container fully back.
5. Feet in footrests.
6. Hands on firing handle.
7. Head hard back on rest.
8. Pull handle over face.
9. Drogue gun fires automatically
10. Auto separation below 10,000ft (Mk 2B seat only).
11. Failure of auto separation (Mk 2B seat only).
    (a) Operate override D-ring.
    (b) Operate seat harness release.
    (c) Raise flap and grasp parachute D-ring.
    (d) Fall clear and pull D-ring.

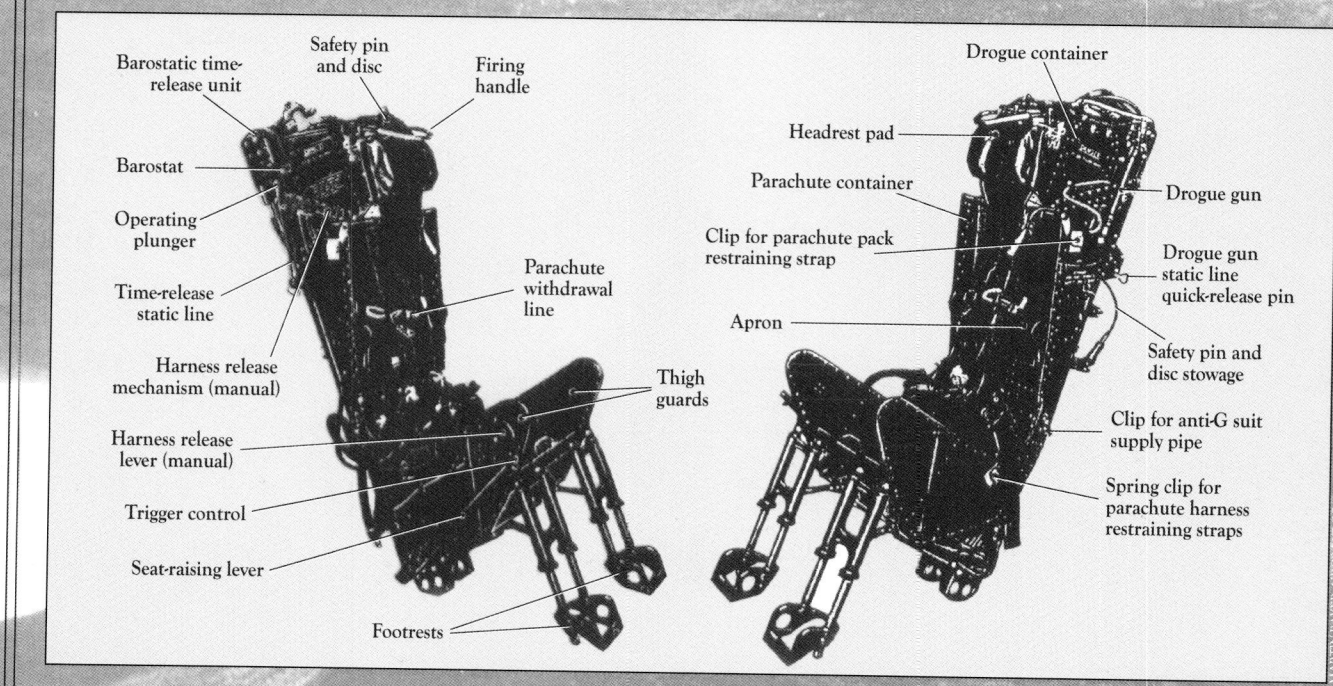

Background image: Three Wyverns from 813 Squadron over mountainous Norwegian terrain during Exercise 'Strikeback', September 1957.

Opposite bottom: The salient features of the Wyvern's Martin-Baker Mk 2B ejection seat.

Right: Lieutenant-Commander 'Smokey' Cowling RN, the Senior Pilot of 830 Squadron, preparing to eject from his Wyvern over the Mediterranean during the Suez hostilities. The aircraft's canopy has already been jettisoned.

Right: Synchronised splashing: a remarkable photograph showing the author hitting the water following his ejection (bottom right) just as his Wyvern, VZ756 (top left), crashes into Harstadtfjord, 24 September 1957.

WYVERN EJECTIONS

Unit	Date	Aircraft	Pilot	Remarks
'C' Sqn A&AEE	08/06/51	VW869	Lt-Cdr D. K. Hanson	Pilot ejected at 1,500ft at high speed but caught left leg on control column. Did not operate manual system. Fatal.
813 NAS/Stretton	07/04/54	VZ779	Lt J. D. Newman	Engine caught fire. Pilot ejected at 7,000ft and 200kts.
813 NAS/*Albion*	13/10/54	VZ783	Lt B. D. MacFarlane	'Cold' catapult shot. Pilot ejected under water, recovered by SAR helicopter.
813 NAS/*Eagle*	12/08/55	WL877	S/Lt A. M. Steers	Engine malfunction. Crashed near Naples.
813 NAS/*Eagle*	14/08/55	VZ778	Lt Bush	Missed arrester wire.
830 NAS/Ford	17/11/55	VZ791	Lt J. P. Smith	Engine malfunction. Following ejection, aircraft belly-landed at Worthy Down.
830 NAS/*Eagle*	17/05/56	WP336	Lt R. King	Aircraft crashed on approach to Hal Far.
830 NAS/*Eagle*	22/05/56	WP339	Lt J. P. Smith	Ejection for reason unknown during carrier landing, circuit 'downwind'. Fatal.
831 NAS/Ford	04/09/56	WN327	Lt R. Sandison	Pilot lost control at low level. Fatal.
830 NAS/*Eagle*	03/11/56	WN330	Lt D. McCarthy	Hit by AA fire. Pilot ejected near carrier, was recovered safely.
830 NAS/*Eagle*	05/11/56	WN328	Lt-Cdr W. H. Cowling	Engine 'exploded' owing to AA fire. Pilot ejected near carrier and was recovered safely.
831 NAS/Ford	17/09/57	VZ795	S/Lt R. W. Edward	Night mid-air collision with VZ798 north of Littlehampton.
831 NAS/Ford	17/09/57	VZ798	S/Lt G. W. Smith	Night mid-air collision with VZ795 north of Littlehampton.
813 NAS/*Eagle*	24/09/57	VZ756	Lt M. J. Doust	Propeller 'Planet' gear failure 100nm north of Arctic Circle. Pilot on 'loan' from 831 NAS.

COURTESY RICHARD L. WARD

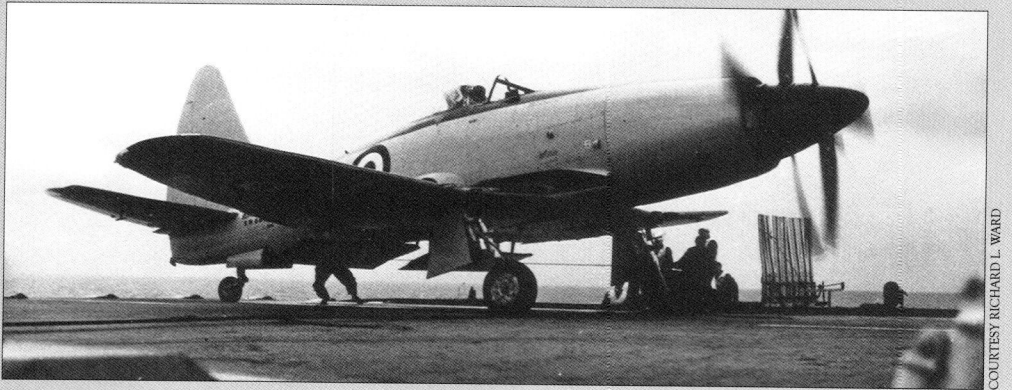

Left: Another photograph taken during the Wyvern's flight-deck trials in 1950–51. This is probably VW867. Below: S. Mk 4 VZ774 seen in 1957 while serving with the Wyvern Conversion Unit. This aircraft is seen in production on page 10 of this book. Bottom: A Wyvern and a Sea Hawk—destined to become shipmates aboard RN carriers—overfly *Ark Royal*, 1955.

COURTESY BRIAN LOWE

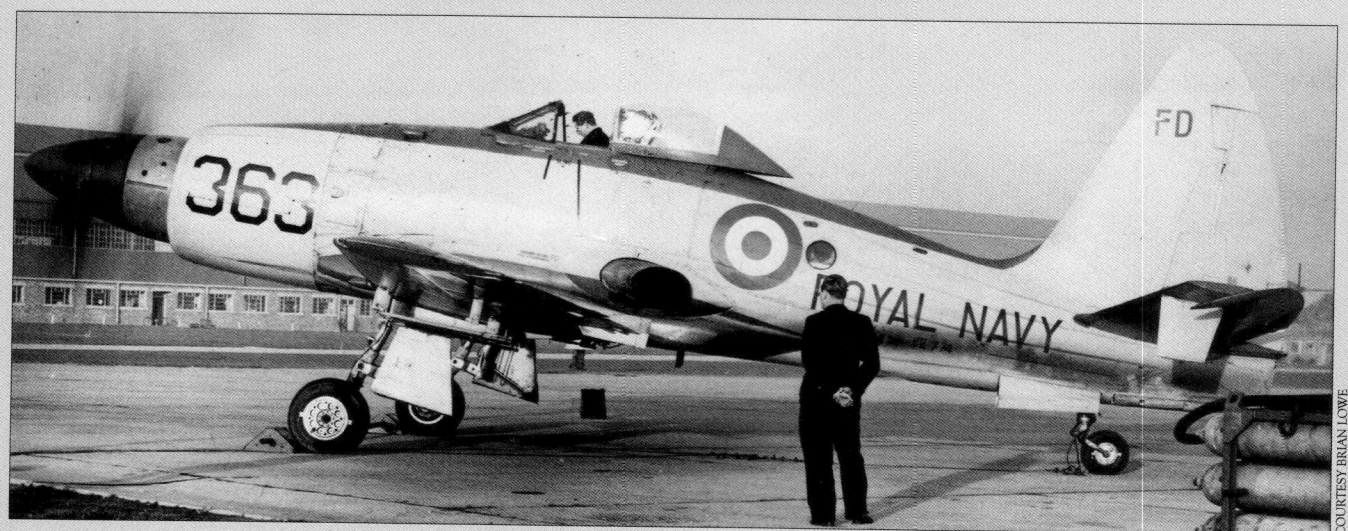

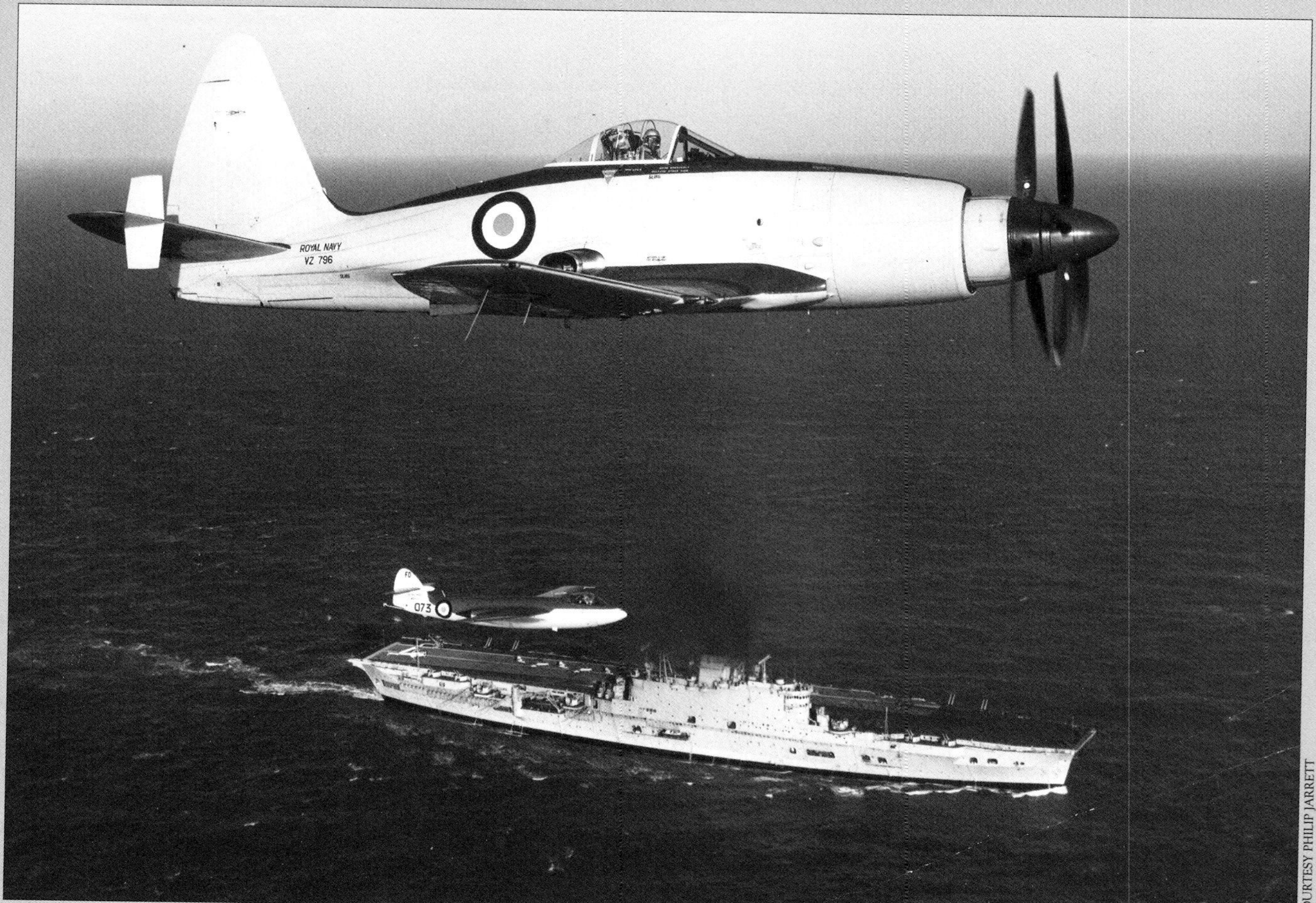

COURTESY PHILIP JARRETT

MORE THAN A LITTLE CHAGRIN
Lieutenant-Commander Robert King MBE RN (RETD)

As with all aircraft, there are many apocryphal stories and the Westland Wyvern, being named after a mythological beast, could well have more of these than most! My association with the aircraft was not of my choosing but it has provided me with many memories—not all pleasant, but all unforgettable.

I was a member of the first RN pilots' course to be awarded 'wings' on jet aircraft at RAF Valley, after which I was appointed to RNAS Lossiemouth to complete Operational Flying Schools (OFS 1 and OFS 2) on Sea Hawks. I could never claim to have been a 'natural' flyer and had to work jolly hard to graduate and qualify as a fighter pilot, and it was, therefore, with more than a little chagrin that I found my next appointment to be to 764 Squadron at RNAS Ford to do a conversion to the Wyvern, which, to be quite honest, was regarded with some dread at that time. I was not alone in being 'selected' for Wyverns: in fact, four more of our passing-out course of ten got the same surprise—and one of these had actually passed out top of our course! Perhaps it was just a coincidence but all five of us had come from the 'lower deck' and trained as Upper Yardmen (Air).

Shortly after I had taken up my new appointment at Ford in June 1955, HMS *Eagle* came into Portsmouth Dockyard with part of a Wyvern's engine embedded in its funnel. This was one of 827 Squadron's aircraft, and was being flown by Lieutenant Jim Jarret on a Deck Landing Practice sortie. When coming over the 'round-down' he was thought to have stalled through pulling too tightly, rolled over and flew into the funnel in an inverted attitude. It must have been at this time that I started hearing apocryphal Wyvern stories.

The first of these, as I recall, supposedly originated in a post-flight report from a Boscombe Down test pilot, which noted that 'Access to the cockpit is difficult; it is recommended that it be made impossible!' In order to enter the aircraft one climbed on to the port main wheel, then up a step which was half-way up the port oleo, then along the wing to the side of the cockpit and thence into the aircraft via footsteps in the side of the fuselage. One of my colleagues, Lieutenant Nigel Anderdon, came to have a chuckle when I had my first go at starting and taxying 'The Beast'. He swears that, as I sat in the cockpit, I said to him, 'I've flown lower than this!' His reply was, 'Check your oxygen connections . . .'

My conversion to the Wyvern was delayed until the first week of August 1955 but then became a very hurried affair as I and two colleagues suddenly received appointments to the two front-line squadrons (813 and 827) that were currently embarked in *Eagle* in the Mediterranean. We were meant to have twenty-five hours on type before joining but only managed about twelve hours each. This meant that we were unable to do deck-landing qualifications, and apart from flying a few times at RAF North Front, Gibraltar, we were condemned to the role of permanent Squadron duty officers—me in 827 (CO Lieutenant-Commander 'Jimmy' Richardson) and Denis McCarthy and George Humphreys in 813 (CO Lieutenant-Commander 'Mike' Crosley).

We came back to home waters and the three hapless 'Musketeers' were 'chopped' ashore to RNAS Brawdy and then flown in a DH Rapide of 781 Squadron to RNAS Ford to try to get some more hours in. We did—but, alas, not enough. From Ford I flew as No 2 to my Squadron Senior Pilot (Lieutenant-Commander Watson) on a freezingly cold flight to Lossiemouth. About two days later *Eagle* arrived in the Moray Firth and we three were now to be allowed to 'deck-qualify'. The weather was pretty awful, with a cloud base of about 500 feet, when Lieutenant 'Charles' Bush, SP of 813, suffered apparent aileron-locking immediately after being launched from the port catapult. He managed to climb away, and upon entering cloud he ejected, knowing that if the Met Man's forecast was correct he now was high enough to do so. The minimums on the seat at that time were 400 feet S&L (straight and level) and at least 120 knots. During the ejection Charles lost the boots from his immersion suit and so he got very wet and very cold before being picked up by the ship's SAR Whirlwind. As a consequence of this accident the Wyvern was temporarily grounded, and so 'we three' were again denied the opportunity to deck-qualify and embarked in *Eagle* by boat once more, this time from Invergordon.

A rather interesting technical detail of the Wyvern that may or may not have had some bearing on the accident to Charles Bush's aircraft was the fact that, by design, when the ejection sequence was initiated the ailerons were locked in the neutral position and the top part of the control column folded forward so that it did not damage the pilot's knees whilst the ejection seat travelled up the guide rails. Because of this, all pilots subsequently had to learn to reassemble the top portion of the stick 'blind', as a safety drill.

Eagle then sailed into the North Sea and the Arctic for a NATO exercise lasting some fourteen days. During this period 827 Squadron lost two more pilots, the first being Lieutenant Mike Teague, who was killed whilst trying to carry out an emergency landing aboard HMS *Bulwark*, and the second the Senior Pilot, Lieutenant-Commander L. P. (Peter) Watson, who ejected whilst in the vicinity of *Eagle* but was dead on being recovered from the sea. Shortly after this, in November 1955, 813 and 827 Squadrons were disbanded at RNAS Ford and some of their aircraft were handed over to the newly formed 830 and 831 Squadrons (Commanding Officers Lieutenant-Commanders Vyvyan Howard and Stan Farquhar, respectively).

The two new squadrons were eventually equipped with brand new, modified Wyvern S. Mk 4 aircraft, which were in many ways nicer to fly—not least of the improvements being the introduction of a clear canopy, giving a very much better all-round visibility from the cockpit. Other modifications included the addition of a large air brake under the fuselage which enabled the pilot to pull out of very steep dives with little physical effort. The folding hinge at the wing-tip section was also deleted, with the result that the pilot did not crack his head when getting out of the cockpit.

What of the 'three musketeers'? We were all appointed to 830 Squadron!

WEAPONS AND TACTICS

WHEN Wyvern pilots flew as a division, they would sortie either as a pair or as a foursome. For a pair of aircraft, the wingman usually flew about a hundred yards out and some 30–45 degrees back, allowing flexibility for manoeuvring and a good arc of vision astern of the leader. In a foursome, the leader of the second pair of aircraft would fly with his section a little further back and a hundred yards out, so that he had clearance of manoeuvre from one side to the other with his wingman.

In ground-attack missions, the approach was almost invariably carried out at low level, pulling up from a predetermined IP (Initial Point) to the roll in attack height, which in most instances was around 2,500 feet AGL (above ground level), into a 20-degree dive. Dive attacks could be as steep as 45 degrees, but this angle was rarely if ever flown; nevertheless, the more steeply one dived, the more accurate would be one's fall of shot (the distance, measured in yards, between the target and the weapon's point of impact). Once the weapon or weapons had been released, the pilot executed a maximum-'g' pull-out, weaving as he left the target area in order to evade any ground anti-aircraft fire. Radar-controlled AA guns always had difficulty tracking an aircraft in a dive because it would be performing a 'bunt', and the shells would therefore be behind it. However, if an AA barrage was set up along the dive-path, there was a high probability that one would be hit—as two pilots of 830 Naval Air Squadron discovered during the Suez confrontation, when their aircraft engines suffered damage and loss of power.

Ground-attack missions generally consisted of rocketing, with 3-inch, 60lb SAP (semi-armour-piercing) warheads, of which the Wyvern was capable of carrying sixteen, or bombing, with either 500- or 1,000-pound HE (high-explosive) bombs. Maritime-attack missions also included mining, with two 1,000-pound sea mines under the wings or a single 2,000-pounder sea mine on the centre weapon station beneath the pilot. In addition, the aircraft had four 20mm cannon, a pair in each wing, with

Below: VW870 demonstrating the weapon load for which the Wyvern was originally designed—a 2,000-pound (18-inch) torpedo. By the time the Wyvern was in production, however, the concept of airborne torpedo attack was fast becoming outmoded, thanks to the improved range and efficiency of shipboard anti-aircraft armament.

Above: A production Wyvern fitted with the aircraft's standard 90-gallon jettisonable underwing tanks.
Right: The 150-gallon centre-line tank was introduced quite late in the Wyvern's career. This sharkmouth-decorated example is seen equipping an 813 Squadron aircraft, WL879. The carriage of external fuel tanks demonstrated the classic trade-off: greater range could only be achieved at the expense of the external weapon load.

120 rounds of either SAP, HE, incendiary or solid ball rounds (for practice) for each gun. In addition, eight 25-pound practice bombs could be carried, four underneath each outboard wing section.

A further capability was photography. The Wyvern could carry F24 cameras in the rear fuselage, with the option of a belly position pointing straight down or a fuselage position, looking either to port or to starboard at an angle of 45 degrees; forward-facing F24s could also, in theory, be carried on the external underwing stations. Each camera port had a cover over it, and when a camera was selected the cover would be automatically ejected, thus revealing the lens. The photograph of the author landing in Harstadtfjord (see page 27) was taken from the port camera in the wingman's aircraft.

Right: Fuel tanks of 150 gallons capacity—mock-ups are shown in the photograph here—were also tested under the wings, but these were not generally introduced to service.

THE ROBERT SANDISON TROPHY

Following the death of Lieutenant Robert Sandison in a low-level ejection from a Wyvern, his father, Colonel Sandison, a Dorsetshire farmer, decided that his family would present a trophy in memory of his son. It would be an annual award, made to the pilot with the most outstanding officer-like qualities and proficiency as a strike pilot. The first recipient was Lieutenant (E)(P) Treavor Spafford, RN. Many years later, in 1965, the author had the honour of being presented with the trophy at RNAS Lossiemouth while he was serving in 800 (Buccaneer) Squadron. It was a very poignant occasion, because Lieutenant Sandison had been a friend of the author, both officers having served in 831 Squadron at RNAS Ford in the late 1950s.

Minelaying was another form of attack to which the Wyvern was ideally suited. These types of sorties would normally be conducted at night against harbours and anchorages. While the author was based at RNAS Ford, arrangements were made with the Rye Harbour Master (who just happened to be his father!) to conduct dummy night attacks against the harbour entrance at low water, using smoke floats. It was essential to have an IP, and the Royal Sovereign Light Vessel was the ideal candidate. In wartime such lights, and for that matter harbour entrance lights, would be extinguished—for obvious reasons. The run-in was made at 250 knots, 100 feet above sea level, using the radio altimeter. The pilots had to concentrate hard on their handling—height, heading, speed, and time—or a violent end and a watery grave could have been the end result. Most of the flares fell in the harbour entrance, but some overshot and landed on Camber Sands—unfortunately to ignite when the tide came in.

Left: Refuelling 830 Squadron Wyverns on board *Eagle* in 1956, the port outer wing tank of the aircraft at left and the starboard jettisonable underwing tank of that on the right being topped up in this photograph. The Wyvern's internal fuel load was distributed amongst seven tanks—main, fuselage rear, fuselage front and inner wing and outer wing port and starboard, the last six feeding fuel to the main tank (that from the wings first passing through the rear fuselage tank) and thence to the engine. A negative 'g' trap in the main tank allowed the pilot fifteen seconds' worth of inverted flight.

WEAPONS AND TACTICS

Right: Various weapon loads were investigated during the development of the Wyvern but not introduced for service use. Installed here are Red Angel air-to-surface rockets, 1954.

In another operation in which full-size dummy mines were used—on this occasion flying from HMS *Ark Royal*—one of the Squadron pilots made a complete hash of his timing and his 2,000-pound centreline load fell with a loud thud in the local postmistress's front garden. It took the Navy a few days to dig out the monster and return the frightened lady's herbaceous border to its original state!

A RARE EVENT

Captain Vyvyan Howard DSC RN

Two general impressions of the Wyvern remain with me: the cockpit layout was very good, all the instruments being easily readable and all controls readily within reach; and the aircraft was comfortable to fly and was a good, steady weapons platform.

During HMS *Eagle*'s 1956 commission 830 Squadron carried out a trial on a proximity-fused bomb, that is, one designed to explode prior to impact in order to create maximum blast and shrapnel effects. We used a 2,000lb bomb—a rare event indeed! There were two of us, with one bomb each. The catapult launch did not seem out of the ordinary, and the climb-away, though a fraction slower than usual, was easily controlled.

A smoke float was launched into the sea a safe distance off the starboard side of the carrier to act as a target, and my wingman—Sub-Lieutenant Parsons, as I remember—and I climbed to somewhere around 10-12,000 feet in good visibility. We spread out so that he could follow me immediately after my bomb had exploded. I turned the aircraft into a 60-degree dive; I recall how smoothly it responded, but the abiding impression remains the continued steadiness of the dive as the Wyvern gained speed. The release height was about 3,000 feet, I guess, with a distinct little upward jerk as the bomb left. The pull-away was normal.

The report on landing was that the accuracy was good and the effect quite spectacular!

Below: A Wyvern of 830 Squadron at RNAS Ford in rather wintry conditions.

Main image: A composite photograph showing Wyvern S.4 WL888 from 830 Naval Air Squadron firing a salvo of 3-inch rockets during a practice shoot.

Forward Air Controlling (FAC) is a mission carried out by both the RN and the RAF over land near enemy lines. All carriers have embarked an FAC team consisting of an officer—usually of Major or Army Captain rank—and half a dozen NCOs and other ranks. The team would be landed ashore, close to the front line, where they would setup a concealed observation post from which they could monitor the enemy's movements, tanks and weapons. The commander of the team would, at the appropriate moment, call in one or more aircraft from an IP and direct them on to the selected target.

The approach to the FAC's position would be made at low level and at between 250 and 350 knots airspeed, pulling up into a steep climb to turn in on the attack heading over the FAC's position or designated turn-in position. The FAC would then talk the Wyvern pilot or pilots down on to the target until they were satisfied that they had located it. The designated weapon or weapons were then fired or dropped, and the FAC would call back to report the success of the attack or otherwise. In certain circumstances he might summon the aircraft back in order to carry out a second attack. This was a dangerous operation as pilots could be subjected to particularly fierce AA and small-arms fire; moreover, the FAC's position, now perhaps revealed, might also come under enemy fire.

WEAPONS AND TACTICS

Above: A close look at the port underwing load of a Wyvern. If underwing tanks were fitted, the space available for rocket rails was halved. This aircraft has protective caps over the muzzles of the 20mm cannon, and a wrap over the pitot tube.
Right: Loading rockets beneath the port wing. Various types of warhead are evident.

It was after such an operation during the Suez Crisis in 1956 that 830 Squadron lost two of its aircraft to AA fire; fortunately, both pilots managed to close their carrier and then eject from their stricken Wyverns, to be picked up safely and without injury by the ship's SAR helicopter. It was following a dummy FAC mission over northern Norway on 24 September 1957, during the NATO exercise 'Strikeback', that the author had to eject from VZ756/'275-J' following a propeller Planet gear failure. Luckily, he was rescued by a couple of Norwegian fishermen and then flown by USAF Albatross SAR amphibian to Andoya airfield at the northern tip of Norway, following which the ship's SAR flew him back to the carrier.

MAINTENANCE

GENERALLY, the Wyvern was an easy aircraft to maintain except for one aspect—the engine! The airframe, controls, electronics, cameras and hydraulics rarely presented any problems to the Squadron maintenance crews, but the engine was something entirely different! The Python engine was originally designed for hauling heavy bombers around the sky—aircraft that would be flying for much of the time straight and level, and, in the main, at a constant airspeed. The Wyvern, on the other hand, was, despite appearances, a fighter aircraft, and would be manœuvring under high 'g' loading during combat. Consequently, the throttle could be moving over the whole of its quadrant quite rapidly throughout much of the sortie. This would cause the engine rpm constant-speeding device to be disturbed, resulting in a loss of constant speed control—and making the pilot's control of the engine difficult to say the least!

Once constant speeding control was lost, the pilot had to handle his engine with kid gloves in order to make a successful approach and landing. If he were making a carrier landing, extreme care was needed in order to carry out a successful approach and touch-down. The same applied at night when landing ashore (the Wyvern was not cleared for night deck landings—which was rather odd, given that the Gannet ASW aircraft *was* cleared).

Resetting the engine constant-speeding control was a long and tedious maintenance chore. 831 Squadron's AEO, Lieutenant (E) (AE) Tony Bastick (who would eventually reach flag rank) was well known for his engine running and testing aboard *Ark Royal*. It was not unusual to receive complaints from the Matron of Binghy Hospital in Malta on a Sunday morning, asking why was there so much noise coming from the flight deck. Could not the ship pick another time, seeing that it was Sunday?

An engine change was in itself quite a straight-forward task, but it was made difficult because the Python had to be lifted by a cradle attached to the top front and rear ends and then slowly nudged on to the forward fire bulkhead of the fuselage. The engine was heavy—weighing in at least two tons or more! At this stage, the contra-rotating propeller mounting was not attached to the engine. It was during the final adjustment, before the propellers were attached, that on one occasion in the author's experience a young air mechanic inadvertently dropped a 2BA wrench near the air intake and lost it. A thorough search was made in and about the air intake but there was no sign of the tool. Eventually the Air Engineering Officer (AEO) reluctantly had

Main image: Wyverns of 813 NAS aircraft at RNAS Ford being prepared for a practice RP strike in 1953 or 1954. Note the propeller-blade locking ties.

COURTESY RICHARD LAVARD

Above: An early-production Wyvern is manœuvred using a Lancing-Bagnall Aircraft Handler. The photograph illustrates why the Wyvern's folding wing tips were so disliked amongst pilots: they were the cause of many a sore head!
Right: Wyvern S.4—probably VZ791/'J', call-sign '129', of 813 Squadron—undergoes engine maintenance 'in the field' in 1955. Note that the jet efflux pipe has been removed.

to give the order for the engine to be removed and sent back to Armstrong Siddeley for a thorough examination. The manufacturers found the wrench at the rear end of the compressor, it having ricocheted from one compressor blade to the next. The whole engine had to be taken down to find it, costing the Navy a huge sum in maintenance fees.

There were various other problems with the engine: for example, when in the early days Wyverns were flying off the carriers' catapults, the engine had cause to fail due to lack of fuel. The problem was resolved at the Royal Aircraft Establishment at Farnborough by the fitting of a recuperator which carried a couple of gallons of fuel. As the aircraft

RECOLLECTIONS OF A PLUMBER–1

Commander John Dunphy RN (RETD)

I was sitting in my office in the Seafire 17 Repair and Modification hangar at RNAS Stretton (HMS *Blackcap*) on a sunny afternoon in spring 1953 when I received a telephone call from the control tower saying. 'It's on its way.' I got into the Tilly and drove over to the tower. In the distance I heard a sound like an angry swarm of bees which gradually swelled into the raucous noise of an overworked coffee-grinder. Out of the haze appeared a shape which resembled that of an overgrown shark. It did several high-speed passes over the airfield and then landed and taxied around the perimeter track to the apron in front of the hangar which was destined to become the Wyvern Receipt and Despatch Unit. It burbled away happily while it was being chocked up, and then the engine stopped and the hood slid back. The Wyvern had arrived.

I stood by the port oleo and looked up in awe. My head was at the level of the wing leading-edge, the cockpit was several feet above and in front were two very large contra-rotating propellers. I stood for a minute or so whilst the pilot was released from the cockpit and my thoughts can be summed up as 'Cor-r-r!' It was big, shiny, and appeared to be built like a battleship. Its resemblance to a shark was due to the sweeping lines of the fuselage, the tall tail fin at the rear and the annular air intake at the front behind the two contra-rotating props.

During the next months a further four or five aircraft were received. The task of the Wyvern RDU was to receive the aircraft on to RN charge, embody Service modifi-cations, carry out acceptance inspections and test flights and prepare the aircraft for despatch to service units. An Armstrong Siddeley service representative, Teddy Kent, joined us at Stretton to help us with any problems that we might experience with the Python constant-speeding turbo-prop engine in the aircraft, which had been the cause of several accidents during its development trials.

On one occasion we were experiencing difficulty with the operation of the air starter on the engine, which was activated by means of a high-pressure air trolley, consisting of a bank of HP air cylinders operated by a three-foot-long lever. Teddy and I took advantage of a quiet Saturday afternoon to carry out some tests and pushed the trolley up to one of the aircraft, uncoiled the fifteen-foot air hose and loosely connected it to the starter. Suddenly the phone rang in the hangar office, and so I asked Teddy to get the starter ready while I was dealing with the call. When I came back he was sitting on the port wing. I asked him if he was ready and he said, 'Yes.' I moved the trolley lever to the 'On' position, there was a loud hiss of escaping air and the air hose snaked out and hit the mainplane leading edge between his knees. I immediately shut off the air and looked at Teddy, who had now gone a ghastly shade of pale green. 'You said you were ready up there.' 'Yes, but I thought that you had already connected the air hose!' We decided to call it a day and returned to the Mess. Teddy Kent was a teetotaller but that afternoon he downed quite a number of 'Horse's Necks' in very short order.

Opposite page: A blemished but nevertheless fascinating photograph of 831 Squadron Wyverns in deep maintenance following disembarkation from *Ark Royal* in 1957.
Left:: VZ750 at the SBAC show at Farnborough, September 1952. The underbelly airborne torpedo shown in this aircraft has the airwing attachment.

accelerated down the catapult, a reversible diaphragm in the recuperator forced the extra fuel into the fuel lines and on to the burners, thereby keeping the engine running.

With the introduction into service of jet-powered aircraft, a new term was created for a phenomenon that might arise while the engines were ground-running—Foreign Object Damage, or FOD. One day a pilot of 830 Squadron was carrying out dummy dives on the ORS circles at Worthy Down near Winchester. As he was pulling out of a dive, his Python quit, forcing him to eject. The fighter flew across a road, just missing some motorists, and belly-landed in a field. The pilot landed safely nearby and was returned to Ford by helicopter, having suffered no injuries. The aircraft was dismantled and taken by the Aircraft Accident Investigation Unit (AAIU) to Lee-on-Solent, where the engine was thoroughly inspected . . . and, lo and behold, a brass button from an air mechanic's jacket was found jammed in the compressor section! It had either fallen into the intake during a routine inspection or had been sucked up from the ground after start-up. The pilot was very lucky to have escaped from the incident unscathed, although, sadly, he would lose his life some months later. He ejected downwind in the carrier recovery circuit, but as neither he nor his aircraft were found, and because there was no radio call, nobody will ever know why.

FLAME-OUT

Captain John Checketts RN (RETD)

A serious problem with the Wyvern during early operations from aircraft carriers was engine flame-out during catapult launch, resulting in the loss of the aircraft. The Naval Air Department of the Royal Aircraft Establishment at Farnborough was therefore tasked to investigate the matter using its airfield-based catapult. One of NAD's main functions was the carrying out of initial catapulting and arresting trials of new naval aircraft in order to determine minimum launch speeds and reveal any basic handling difficulties, prior to formal carrier trials by the Naval Test Squadron at the Aircraft and Armament Experimental Establishment at Boscombe Down as part of the full release procedure for the aircraft. Initial trials of the Wyvern by NAD had not, apparently, revealed any problems.

In 1954–55 an intensive programme of launches of a Wyvern was conducted by NAD in co-operation with Westland Aircraft, Armstrong Siddeley (the Python engine manufacturer) and Dowty (the fuel pump manufacturer). The test aircraft, VZ782, was fitted with instrumentation to record fuel pressure and flow during catapult launch in the long fuel pipe between the engine and the pump in the main fuel tank behind the cockpit. The pilot was not allowed to fly the aircraft away from the catapult after launch but required to close the throttle and land directly on the runway ahead. An engine flame-out eventually occurred, brought about by the reduced flow in the main fuel pipe during the launch stroke.

As a result of these trials, fuel delivery to the engine was improved by increasing the output pressure from the fuel pump, but the main solution was the fitting of a two-gallon-capacity recuperator: during the launch stroke the acceleration caused a reversible diaphragm in the recuperator to force extra fuel into the system, thus keeping the engine running.

Below: Wyvern VZ776 demonstrating a flame-out, probably during proof and barrier trials at RAE Farnborough in 1954.

SHIPS AND SQUADRONS

THE first two Wyvern squadrons to be commissioned were 813 NAS and 827 NAS, which were equipped with the aircraft from May 1953 to November 1955 and were based at, respectively, RNAS Ford (HMS *Peregrine*), near Arundel, and RNAS Stretton (HMS *Blackcap*), in Lancashire. Each squadron was equipped with nine aircraft, and they embarked in HM Ships *Albion* and *Eagle*; the latter's near-sister ship HMS *Ark Royal*, was in deep refit at Devonport Dockyard at the time. It was while *Eagle* was embarking her Wyverns off the Isle of Wight that one stalled over the flight deck and crashed upside-down into the ship's funnel. The pilot, Lieutenant Jim Jarret, was severely injured and never flew fixed-wing aircraft again Unfortunately, as a result of various other accidents, nine of the two squadrons' eighteen aircraft were lost, and a number of pilots were, tragically, killed.

When *Eagle* returned to home waters, 813 and 827 were decommissioned and two further squadrons, 830 and 831, were resurrected from wartime days and commissioned at Ford during November 1955. By mid-1956 *Eagle* was due to recommission, and since *Ark Royal* remained in refit it was decided by Their Lordships, that their 'strike eggs' should not, on this occasion, be embarked all in one ship. It was decided, therefore, that both Squadron Commanding Officers, Lieutenant-Commanders Howard (830), and Farquhar (831)

Right: The first of the Royal Navy's aircraft carriers to embark Wyverns were *Albion* (upper) and *Eagle* (lower); *Ark Royal* would be the third.

Main image: A Wyvern catches the wires aboard *Eagle*.

would visit Flag Officer Flying Training, Admiral 'Crash' Evans, at Yeovilton to discuss and decide which squadron would go to sea first. A coin was tossed and Stan Farquhar lost: 830 Squadron embarked aboard *Eagle* and 831 remained ashore until *Ark Royal* was ready for sea.

813 NAVAL AIR SQUADRON

'Full Sails'

Commission	Commanding Officer	Senior Pilot	AEO
03/03/53–21/11/55	Lt-Cdr S. S. Laurie (03/03/53)	Lt-Cdr E. T. Genge	Lt (E) D. G. Rowles
	Lt-Cdr C. E. Price (18/05/53)		
	Lt-Cdr R. M. Crosley (15/12/54–21/11/55)	Lt-Cdr D. M. Searson	
26/11/56–22/04/58	Lt-Cdr R. W. Halliday (26/11/56)	Lt-Cdr F. J. Golightly	Lt-Cdr D. J. Turner
	Lt-Cdr R. W. T. Abraham (02/12/57)	Lt-Cdr Matthews	—do—

Main image: Hook down, VZ783/'197-Z' approaches touch-down, probably in the carrier *Albion* (to which the Squadron was assigned in mid-1954) since the tailwheel appears not to be locked. This is the aircraft from which Lieutenant MacFarlane made the world's first underwater ejection.

Above left: VZ781 ashore at RNAS Hal Far, Malta, in late 1954.

Above right: Final checks at Hal Far, late 1954. The Squadron crest is displayed on the upper fuselage just forward of the cockpit.

Below: During its commissions the 813 tail code progressed from 'Z' (HMS *Albion*) through 'J' to 'E' (both HMS *Eagle*). Here, during the Squadron's final commission, VZ750 departs as '766 sits on *Eagle*'s starboard bow catapult.

Above: VZ753/'183' in 1953-54. The aircraft has twin stripes in red and yellow around the outer wings and rear fuselage—special markings applied for Exercise 'Mariner' in autumn 1953—and royal blue spinners and upper 'finlets' (doubtless outboard only).
Left: A very smart VZ787: the 813 CO's machine *circa* June 1955, with royal blue spinners and white-striped royal blue 'finlets'.

LAST LAUNCH

Commander R. W. T. Abraham RN (RETD)

I was the CO of the last Wyvern squadron, 813 NAS, embarked in HMS *Eagle* and with its home base at RNAS Ford in Sussex.

The Wyvern was a strong and robust aircraft and an excellent weapon platform; unfortunately, it was a little late in entering service and the jets overtook it in terms of performance and handling as well as being much easier to deck-land. Having said that, it is only fair to add that the Wyvern, given the respect it deserved, was pleasant to handle on the approach and subsequent landing. One of its drawbacks was the wing leading edge: if this were dented or damaged, the stalling speed of the aircraft could be affected by five knots or so. Because of this, some pilots not flying their own designated machine would check the stalling speed of the aircraft before approaching the deck.

One other thing of note was that the Wyvern had a lockable tailwheel—which was used when landing ashore on airfields. If one forgot to lock the wheel it invariably resulted in quite severe tail 'shimmy'. It was never used in deck landings as it was quite unnecessary when flying into the arresting wires.

The last launch of 813 Squadron from *Eagle* was on 27 March 1958. This took place in the Channel on our return from the Med. We landed at Ford, refuelled and flew on to RNAS Lossiemouth, where the aircraft were stored pending their eventual removal for scrapping. On launch from *Eagle* I was sent a signal from Flag Officer Aircraft Carriers saying, 'I am not sorry to see the Wyvern go, but I shall miss its cheerful and competent pilots.'

Left: A Wyvern of 813 Squadron on board *Eagle* during its last commission. The well-known bomb-riding 'Dennis the Menace' artwork adorns the starboard fuselage, and the fin code letter—now 'E' for *Eagle* instead of 'J'—is of reduced size.

827 NAVAL AIR SQUADRON

'Ya Mansur Amit'

Commission	Commanding Officer	Senior Pilot	AEO
01/11/54–19/11/55	Lt-Cdr S. J. A. Richardson	Lt-Cdr C. V. Gregory	Lt (E) L. F. Collishaw

Left: A scene aboard *Eagle* in May or June 1955, during 827 Squadron's sole commission at sea. The Squadron's adoption of the wyvern emblem is prominently proclaimed on the Wyverns' starboard engine cowlings. *Eagle*'s SAR Dragonfly helicopter is visible on the port deck-edge.

Left: The Squadron was joined by 813 for its deployment at sea, three of the latter unit's aircraft appearing in the foreground of this photograph. The 827 aircraft are parked on *Eagle*'s starboard quarter, together with, furthest forward, a Wyvern that appears to have 'jumped' from 813 since it retains the latter's smaller tail code letter and appears to have had its wyvern emblem (not very subtly) painted out. Gannet A.S. Mk 1s of 826 Squadron—whose first deployment this was with the aircraft—are parked opposite.

FORTY-FOUR

SHIPS AND SQUADRONS

Above: An appalling accident befell 827 on board *Eagle* on 17 May 1955 as the ship was embarking the Squadron's Wyverns. Lieutenant Jim Jarret crashed into the ship's funnel while landing-on and was badly injured as a result; he was trapped in the wreckage for fifteen minutes. This image shows the aftermath of the accident: a fork-lift truck is clearing away the port wing, part of the outer section of which remains embedded half way up the funnel (the under-wing roundel can just be made out).

Right: Happier days: 827 'on board' HMS *Peregrine* (alias RNAS Ford), shortly after the Squadron recommissioned with Wyverns on 1 November 1954.

FORTY-FIVE

830 NAVAL AIR SQUADRON

'In Via Gloriæ'

Commission
21/11/55–05/01/57

Commanding Officer
Lt-Cdr C. V. Howard

Senior Pilot
Lt-Cdr W. H. Cowling

AEO
Lt (AE) J. Dunphy

COVERED WITH OIL!

Captain Vyvyan Howard DSC RN

An incident that remains in my mind is an emergency landing on *Eagle*. The carrier was sailing into a breezy, white-horse sea, and I was conducting a low-level exercise sortie. There was a slight salt spray in the wind. Between the two contra-rotating airscrews of the Wyvern was an oil seal, and on this occasion mine chose to fracture. Suddenly I had no forward vision, the windscreen having quickly become covered with a mix of oil and salt!

I pulled up and informed the carrier, which went to Recovery Stations and, wisely, left me until last to land-on. I could see perfectly well out of the side windows, but straight-ahead visibility was zero. I got into the landing curve quite normally, but as I straightened up on finals I lost sight not only of the landing indicator but also of the deck itself. I was therefore talked down by the Lieutenant-Commander (Flying), one Bertie Birse, on the flying bridge. When he told me to cut the engine I landed slap in the middle of the wires.

However, on this of all occasions the hook bounced and missed all the wires. At the shout in my earphones of 'Round again—full throttle!' I pushed the throttle lever fully forward. The engine responded beautifully and I was airborne again.

The second time around we used the same procedure and Bertie Birse, an experienced aviator and cool as a cucumber, talked me down again. He landed me once more in the middle of the wires, and this time the hook connected.

A reliable aeroplane with a superbly laid-out cockpit had made the emergency easier to handle than it might have been—but there is no doubt that I owe the rest of my life to Bertie Birse.

Main image: Coming up on *Eagle*'s after lift preparatory to a sortie. In the lift well, the 830 Squadron AEO, Lieutenant John Dunphy (back to camera), and the Duty Officer, Lieutenant J. P. Smith, check that all is proceeding smoothly. Much to the relief of Wyvern pilots, the folding wing tips had by this time been dispensed with.
Left: A pair of 830 Squadron Wyverns; one is fitted with jettisonable tanks. The 'finlets' of 830's aircraft were for much of their service finished in royal purple (often referred to as 'maroon') with a golden yellow stripe or stripes (the Senior Pilot's aircraft having two and the CO's three). These colours are confirmed by John Dunphy, one of the contributors to this book: he was the officer who physically mixed the paint!

RECOLLECTIONS OF A PLUMBER—2

Commander John Dunphy RN (RETD)

In the middle of 1953 I left Stretton and did a two-year Post Graduate Course in Engine Design at the College of Aeronautics Cranfield, and obtained a Master of Science Degree. When the course finished I was appointed to 830 Squadron in the hope that my engine design capabilities could in some way assist with the resolution of any further problems which might be experienced. 830 formed up at RNAS Ford in autumn 1955, but deliveries of the first new Wyverns were delayed and we were allocated the aircraft from 827 Squadron when it disembarked from HMS *Eagle* in November 1955 and disbanded. The 827 aircraft were well-used vehicles, and on landing at Ford they taxied to the Squadron hangar, were towed inside and subsided in a heap of unserviceabilities and defects. One aircraft had a piece of tinplate pop-riveted to the leading edge of the port wing and a note in the Form A.700 informing us of a 'Temporary repair carried out to enable aircraft to disembark—not to be flown again until properly repaired.' After much hard work we managed to get most of the aircraft serviceable and the pilots started getting some experience in flying them.

In December 1955 Lt J. P. Smith was carrying out dummy dive attacks at Worthy Down when his engine failed and he had to eject. The aircraft flew on and made a reasonably satisfactory wheels-up landing on farmland near Winchester. The subsequent investigation revealed that there had been foreign object damage to the engine compressor. The Python engine had double skinned clamshell engine doors with a 4-5-inch space between the inner and outer skins. The Accident Investigators discovered a pair of Wrens' service-issue knickers, known as 'blackouts', in the void between the two skins and descended upon 830 Squadron to investigate whether there had been any 'goings on' in the hangar during the night watches. In the event we were able to prove to them that the offending article had come from a bale of waste supplied to the Squadron for cleaning purposes, and the matter was closed.

The experience of rectification on the former 827 aircraft indicated that the maintenance load would be very high when we embarked. Our brand new aircraft arrived in November–December 1955, and we completed Acceptance Inspections and started flying with a hectic programme of familiarisation and ADDLs (Aerodrome Dummy Deck Landings). We then went on Christmas leave and on returning to the hangar—which we shared with 831 Squadron—we found a scene of carnage. The hangar was littered with aircraft with engines removed and wires and pipes hanging out of them. Our engines had been put in Engine Stands. In my office there was a note from Tony Bastick, AEO 831 Squadron, who had formed a Retard party saying, 'Welcome back. All your engines have to be changed, so I have removed them for you. Hope you had a good Christmas.' Replacement engines arrived a day or two later, we reassembled the aircraft and life resumed its normal pattern for Wyvern squadrons—i.e., hectic routine and hard graft.

Leading Pilots' Mates formed an important part of the maintenance team and they were assigned to individual aircraft; the individual aircraft were notionally assigned to individual pilots. An AFO was issued defining the duties and responsibilities of Pilot's Mates and ending with a short paragraph informing the reader that 'aircrew are to be encouraged to be intimate with the Pilot's Mates to ensure a close degree of familiarity with the aircraft and *esprit de corps*.' This caused much conversation at the bar: 'It's all right for the shore-based squadrons who have got Wren Pilots' Mates, but *we* would be prosecuted for this!' etc.

Each aircraft had its own servicing team comprising a Pilot's Mate and two Naval Airmen. When the aircraft was serviceable it was moved out to the line ready to fly and the servicing team carried out the refuelling and pre-flight servicing under the supervision of the Line Chief (Air Fitter). When unserviceable the aircraft would be returned to the hangar and the servicing team would assist the Squadron Hangar Party (composed mainly of Aircraft Artificers) to carry out the repairs. Thus if an aircraft flew on an early sortie and then throughout the day and went U/S towards the end of the day rectification would have to be carried out during the night hours, and the team would have a very long working day.

In April 1956 we embarked in HMS *Eagle* and the maintenance team began familiarising themselves with life and working practices on an aircraft carrier. The aircraft tended to be flown throughout the day and rectified and serviced at night in order to be ready for the next day. The Squadron did not have enough maintenance men to work in two watches and so long hours were worked in hot conditions by most of the personnel.

When the ship visited Mediterranean ports, for example Gibraltar, Malta, Toulon, Istanbul and Naples, the maintenance team would be working on the aircraft to get them ready for the next period at sea whilst the off-duty watch of the ship's company took shore leave. It appeared that the reputations of the Squadron COs in the eyes of Their Lordships was dictated by the number of flying hours that they would extract from their aircraft, and this resulted in pressure on the AEOs to achieve the highest possible aircraft serviceability. Frequently the maintenance men's lot was not a happy one.

The Python and the contra-prop assembly had very short lives between overhauls, which were carried out by return to manufacturer. Both were heavy and ungainly items to handle in the hangar, and their removal and installation, together with the periodic Minor Inspections, reduced the hours of aircraft availability significantly. For a period of a month or two a series of oil seal leaks occurred, causing serious oil spillage over the front windscreen of aircraft in flight and creating very hazardous situations when attempting to deck-land the aircraft with impaired forward visibility. The problem was eventually traced to a batch of imperfect propeller seals which had been supplied for installation. On flying days aircraft had to be ranged from the upper and lower hangars up to the flight deck by means of the aircraft lifts. Any aircraft that landed unserviceable had to be struck down to the hangars on the lifts for repairs, and serviceable aircraft had to be sent up on the lifts to the flight deck to replace them for the next flight. All the aircraft movements in the hangars and the lifts were accomplished by large teams of men using muscle power and this impeded the progress of rectification of aircraft in the hangars.

In May 1956 tragedy struck. I was on the flight deck talking to the Flight Deck Officer and watching a returning flight of Wyvern aircraft which were flying down wind on the port side of the carrier at a height of about 300-400 feet when we heard shouts, looked up, and saw that a Wyvern, piloted by Lieutenant J. P. Smith, which had been abreast the carrier was floating nose down in the water. The SAR helicopter was quickly on the scene, assisted by a seaboat, and hoisted the pilot on board and brought him back to Eagle's Sick Bay but unfortunately he was dead. It appeared that he had attempted to eject from the aircraft but it had hit the water before he was clear of the windscreen assembly. Initially this event was put down to 'another of the Python failures', but I had talked to one of the SAR helicopter's crewmen who mentioned to me that there did not seem to be much if any fuel in the sea around the wreckage. I impounded the aircraft servicing Form A700 and looked through it. All seemed well, and the aircraft had taken off with a full load of fuel, which had been signed for by the pilot. It then transpired that shortly after the aircraft was launched the pilot reported that he appeared to have a fuel system defect but that he intended to fly using his wingman's fuel gauges based on the assumption that both aircraft had been full of fuel and were carrying out the same sortie together. I obtained the form A700 for the other aircraft and coincidentally both aircraft had flown as a pair on the three sorties together on that day. Comparing the fuel states of the aircraft it appeared that throughout the day the crashed aircraft had about 170 gallons less fuel put in than the aircraft which had successfully landed—which had some 170 gallons left in its tank. I deduced that the aircraft probably crashed due to lack of fuel when completing its last sortie.

This theory was accepted by the Board of Inquiry, and it was concluded that as the crashed aircraft fuel gauges had indicated 'full' when prepared for its last flight, and as the pilot had presumably checked his fuel state before taking off, a defect had occurred in the fuel gauging system and this defect probably caused the main fuel gauges to register 'full' when in fact they were only partially full. The pilot on the preceding flight claimed that the aircraft was serviceable for flight when he landed it and that the refuelling operation was carried out and supervised in accordance with the procedures laid down.

This was a tragedy that should never have occurred, and it was being further investigated when the Suez Crisis started to develop. The aircraft itself was not recovered for investigation; all the evidence was purely circumstantial and remains so to this day.

On returning to Malta after a period at sea we were to disembark most of the aircraft on board to RNAS Hal Far to carry on the flying programme from the air station. In readiness for disembarkation some 30-40 aircraft—Sea Hawks, Gannets, Skyraiders and Wyverns—were ranged on the aft end of Eagle's flight deck waiting to fly off. At the front end of the flight deck a Wyvern was adjacent to the starboard catapult and a Sea Hawk sat on the port catapult. The Wyvern was moved a few yards back from the catapult to allow the HP starter trolley to be used. The usual flurry of activity was in progress on the flight deck when the green light went on in Flyco and over the tannoy came the order 'Start turning and burning'. As propellers started whirling and jet pipes exuded kerosene fumes, I checked that my five Wyverns at the after end of the flight deck had started satisfactorily. I then extricated myself from this scene of noise and fumes and went up to the front end of the flight deck to look at the Wyvern which was sitting by the starboard catapult with the HP trolley attached. All was quiet—very quiet. The Pilot's Mate was looking very concerned and he told me that the aircraft was all right but that there didn't seem to be a pilot for it. The Squadron Duty Officer appeared and I told him to find out where the pilot was and to get him up to the aircraft as quickly as his little legs would carry him. The Flight Deck Officer (Lieutenant-Commander Johnny Culbertson) came over to me and asked me what the —— hell was going on, and I told him that we seemed to be suffering from a pilot deficiency. He asked me to start the aircraft up so that the air starter trolley could be moved back to safety in the lee of the island so I hopped in and started up. I was then asked to move the aircraft a few yards forward to its normal spot for catapult take-off in order to save time. I also carried out engine tests ready for take-off.

At this point the Flight Deck Officer's choleric face appeared at the cockpit and he advised me that war seemed to have broken out on the bridge and Flyco because we had held the disembarkation up for about ten minutes. He asked me if I had my copy of Pilot's Notes in my overalls and I reassured him that I had. He told me that I'd better —— well read them because if a pilot didn't turn up within a few minutes 'you will be flying the —— aircraft to Hal Far yourself!' At this moment Lieutenant Bob King emerged from the island and struggled up the flight deck pulling on his flying overalls over his pyjamas. I dismounted, and he got in. The engine roared into take-off power and the aircraft accelerated down the catapult. I understand that there was some discussion between Commander (Air) and the pilot a little later on.

A couple of weeks later I was sitting in the Line Office at Hal Far when the 'phone rang and I was advised that a Wyvern piloted by Lieutenant Bob King was circling the airfield with an undercarriage problem. It appeared that when he had selected 'Undercarriage Down' one leg had gone into the 'Locked Down' position whilst the other remained 'Locked Up'. I collected an assortment of books and drawings containing details of the undercarriage system and went over to the control tower where I met the Senior Pilot (Lieutenant-Commander 'Smokey' Cowling). We advised the pilot over the radio to operate the 'Emergency Down' selector, which should have blown the undercarriage down using an HP air bottle. This was to no avail. The SP advised him to bump the aircraft down on the runway in an attempt to dislodge the jammed leg, but this, too, was to no avail. By this time I had looked through the aircraft drawings and had come to the conclusion that due to the arrangement of micro-switches and sequence valves the leg that was up would not come down until the leg that was down came up and that the leg that was down couldn't go up until the leg that was up came down. An attempt to ditch the aircraft in the sea with an undercarriage leg hanging down or doing a one-wheel-down landing on the runway could be injurious to the pilot's health! The pilot was therefore advised to regain altitude for a safe ejection, point the aircraft away from the coastline into the Mediterranean, wait for the SAR helicopter to join him and eject when he was ready. This he did quite safely. The aircraft continued out to sea for a few miles and then turned round and came back to the coastline, finally splashing down not far from Birzebuggia Bay.

THE FREDS

Lieutenant-Commander Robert King MBE RN (RETD)

During 830 Squadron's shore work-up period at Ford there came the phase in the programme that was devoted to weapons delivery at the nearby air-to-sea range at Bracklesham Bay. 831 Squadron 'got one up' on 830 and was the first to receive its range call-signs— 'Alpha, 'Bravo' and so on. However, had the sequence been adopted 'Vyv' Howard, the CO, would have been allocated the call-sign 'Juliet', and this would only have happened over his dead body. Instead, therefore, the entire Squadron took on the call-sign 'Fred', the CO being 'Fred 1', the Senior Pilot 'Fred 2' and so on down the line of seniority until we got to Sub-Lieutenant Charles Parsons, an Old Etonian whom the two COs decided should have the call-sign 'Charlie'. Thus from that time onwards 830 Squadron was known throughout the Fleet Air Arm as the 'Freds'. In total there were ten 'Freds' and one 'Charlie'.

Came April 1956 and Their Lordships decided that only one of the two new Wyvern squadrons would embark in *Eagle*, and so, at the end of April, 830 embarked and sailed for the Mediterranean. The first port of call was of course Gibraltar, and then we went on to Malta, arriving there in early May. 830 was to disembark six aircraft to RNAS Hal Far (HMS *Falcon*) to continue work-up and weapons training.

It was during this period of disembarked flying at Hal Far that I had cause to confirm the efficacy of the Martin-Baker ejection seat. Nothing really exciting until *le moment critique*: I had been firing rockets on the range at Delimara, and on returning to the Hal Far circuit I selected the undercarriage 'down' but only the starboard leg descended, the port unit remaining firmly locked 'up'. After much chin-scratching among the 'sages' and very many suggestions as to what I should do next, I was eventually ordered to climb on a south-easterly heading to 8,000 feet and then to eject.

After some 60 to 70 minutes of orbiting, selecting the gear 'down' whilst flying inverted etc. and knowing all the time that eventually I should have to eject, actually pulling the handle and finding myself suspended under a parachute at 8,000 feet was something of an anti-climax.

Having entered the water, I experienced another of life's weird coincidences. The SAR Dragonfly had been launched from Hal Far and was almost ready, waiting to winch me up on board,. The pilot of the helicopter was Lieutenant 'Bruce' McFarlane, a New Zealander who was the first, and as far as I know the only, person to carry out a successful underwater ejection, in anger—and that was, believe it or not, from a Wyvern of 813 Squadron from HMS *Albion*.

With the Air Group re-embarked, *Eagle* went on a 'showing the flag' tour of the Med. The ports visited included Istanbul, Beirut, Naples and Toulon, after which we returned to Malta in late July to disembark some aircraft, largely for night flying practice. The disembarkation launch was to start at 0630, and six Wyverns of 830 Squadron were to be joined by six Gannets of 812 for a 'Balbo' flypast. I was to be one of the participants as 'Fred 6' in the second 'vic' of the formation.

Regrettably, when called in the morning I failed to arise immediately and eventually was reawoken by an irate duty officer at about 0625. Unusually, it had been decided to launch the Wyverns first and, unfortunately, my aircraft had been spotted on the starboard catapult. In my absence the Squadron Air Engineer Officer, Lieutenant John Dunphy, had bravely got into the cockpit and started the engine. It took me but a few seconds to arrive from my cabin on 'six' deck (6X13)—situated as far aft and as far below the flight deck as was possible. John and I quickly swapped places, though not before five Wyverns and a Gannet had been launched from the port catapult. Apparently the airwaves on 'Flyco' frequency were quite blue as Commander (Air)—Commander 'Barry' Nation—ranted on at the pilot of Wyvern '376', although I was quite oblivious to all this as John had not switched the radios on and I was too busy getting into my 'slot' in the formation before the 'Balbo' went past the ship. My fools' paradise did not last long, however, as Commander (Air) flew ashore in a 'chopper' and told me, it seemed many times over, who I was and what I was and what I could expect if I committed any further misdemeanour. As it was, I was required on board for duty for the next seven days!

It was after re-embarking from Hal Far again later in the year that we lost another one of our aircraft and, tragically, the pilot too. This was Lieutenant J. P. Smith, one of the few of the junior officers who was married at that time. 'Jape' was the leader of a sortie of three aircraft, and shortly after take-off he reported a fuel gauge problem. Whilst flying on the downwind leg at 400, his engine stopped, and, although he ejected, he died in the accident. 'Jape' had previously ejected from a Wyvern at Worthy Down ORS Range from one of the 'older', former 813 Squadron aircraft which had the ribbed canopy through which one was not supposed to be able to eject!

Right: WN328 wearing three stripes to denote the CO's aircraft. However, this was also the aircraft from which 830's Senior Pilot, Lieutenant Cowling, ejected during the Suez Crisis—see page 27.

SHIPS AND SQUADRONS

Above: 'The Freds'—as handsome a group of aviators as ever there was. (Front row, left to right) John Webster, George Humphreys, Vyvyan Howard (CO), Denis McCarthy, Stan Roddick, George Barras, Eric Hobbs (ALO); (back row, left to right) Bob King, John Dunphy (AEO), Charles Parsons, W. H. 'Smokey' Cowling, Derek Scott, Peter McKern.

Above: WN326, its royal purple finlets with two golden yellow stripes signifying the SP's aircraft, catches the wires aboard *Eagle*. The main wheels are inches away from making contact with the flight deck. Left: WP337/'378-J' is 'squirted' off *Eagle*'s port forward catapult for a practice sortie over the Mediterranean. This photograph makes an interesting comparison with that on page 19 showing early flight-deck trials on board the same ship.

FIFTY-ONE

831 NAVAL AIR SQUADRON

'Aquila Non Capit Muscas'

Commission
21/11/55–10/12/57

Commanding Officer
Lt-Cdr S. C. Farquhar

Senior Pilot
Lt-Cdr W. A. 'Jock' Tofts
Lt-Cdr P. Swithinbank

AEO
Lt A. Bastick
Lt Coxhead

Above: Unfolding his aircraft's wings, Lieutenant-Commander Stan Farquhar leads out 831 Squadron for a flypast over NAS Ford in 1956.

Left: Another fine body of naval aviators—831 Squadron officers on commissioning in November 1955: (front row, left to right) George Wilcox (ALO), Pete Wheatley, 'Jock' Tofts (SP), Stan Farquhar (CO), Gus Gray, Tony Bastick (AEO); (back row, left to right) Mike Doust, unremembered, Bobby Sandison, Reg Hunt, Mike Smith, Treavor Spafford, Gerry McFall.

Below: 831 *En route* for a Squadron take-off, Ford, 1956.

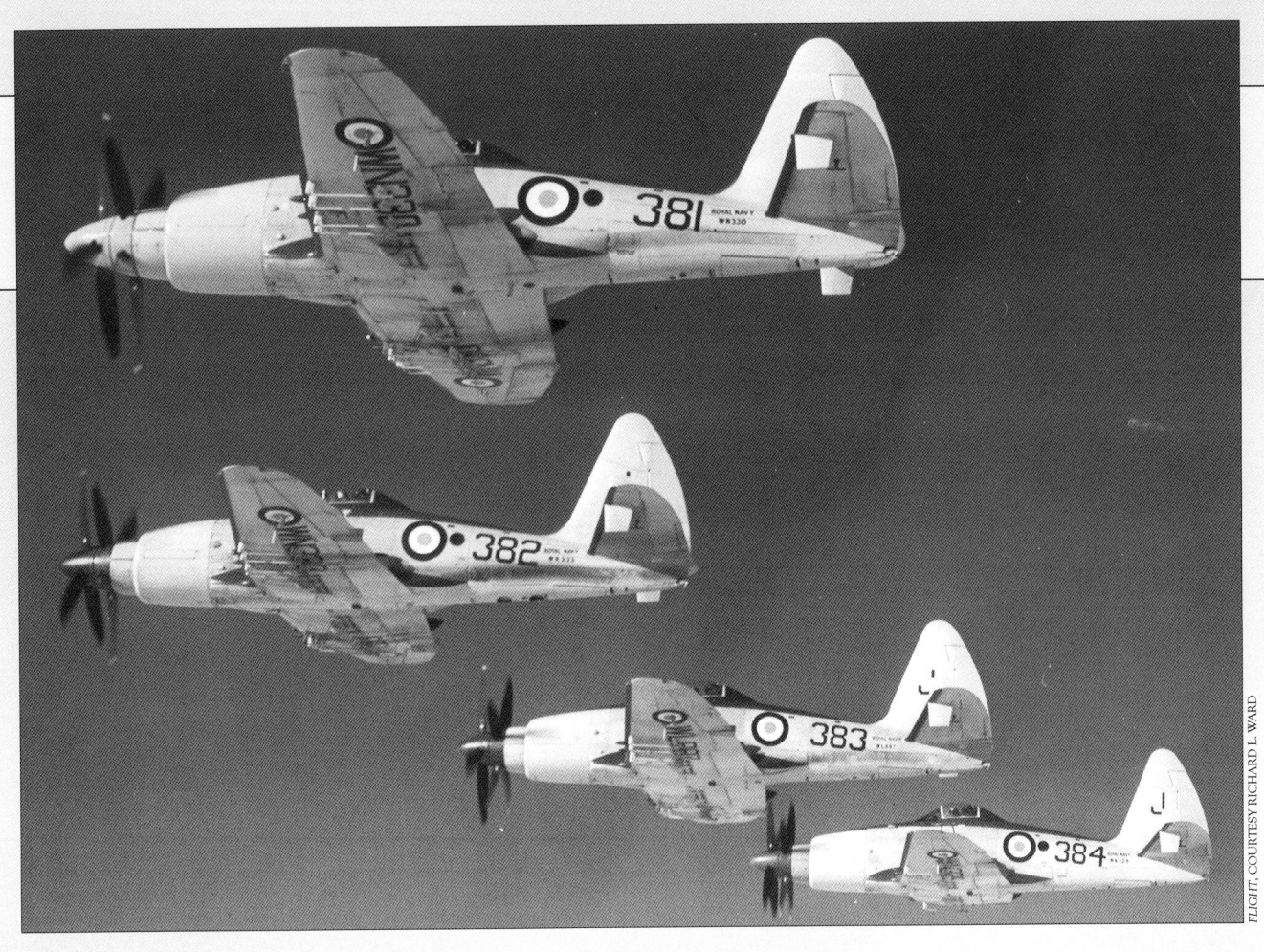

Above: Despite here showing 'J-for-Eagle', 831 never flew from that carrier. In late 1955, with *Ark Royal* in refit, only *Eagle* was able to embark a new Wyvern squadron following the decommissioning of 813 and 827 Squadrons, and Wyvern folklore has it that the decision as to whether this should be 830 or 831 NAS was decided on a toss of the coin between the two units. Fact or legend, in the event 831 only ever embarked on *Ark Royal* ('O'). This photograph of an 831 foursome up from Ford was taken on 22 February 1956; the author is flying '381'.

Left: 831 Squadron's Wyverns aboard *Ark Royal* in 1957. A pair of dark-painted AEW Skyraiders are seen aft, with a pair of Gannets behind them.

FIFTY-THREE

THE STORY OF FLOOK
The Author

In the summer of 1956 Treavor Spafford and I decided that 831's Wyverns—or, at least, one of them—needed some decoration. Treavor was friendly with Wally Fawkes, a British-Canadian jazz musician—and, yes, a descendant of Guy!—who, under the pseudonym 'Trog', was responsible for the the *Daily Mail* cartoon strip 'Flook'. We hatched a scheme, Wally gave his blessing, Treavor and I prepared a 'rough' on a large sheet of cardboard, and at about 1800 one evening, having had a 'nod' from the CO, and with furtive glances all round, we stole out to the line and set about our task.

The SP was unimpressed, but eventually he relented, though insisted that no other aircraft be enhanced in this way. As can be seen from various photographs in this book, however, in due course virtually the entire complement of 831 Wyverns was similarly adorned.

In 1957, with the change in the presentation of FAA aircraft markings—the 'Royal Navy' legend being much increased in size and the aircraft call-signs being shifted as a result to the engine cowlings—'Flook' was moved further back along the starboard fuselage, to a position beneath the cockpit. The character was, as far as I am aware, always presented in black and white: certainly that is how I painted 'Jock' Toft's aircraft: colour cartoon strips in national newspapers were rather a long way in the future in those days!

Below, left and right: The author and Pete Wheatley put the finishing touches to the SP's aircraft. Treavor Spafford is in the cockpit and Captain Wathall and Stan Farquhar pose with the template.
Bottom: A 'Flooked' Wyvern, WN325, comes to grief on board *Ark Royal* in late 1957.

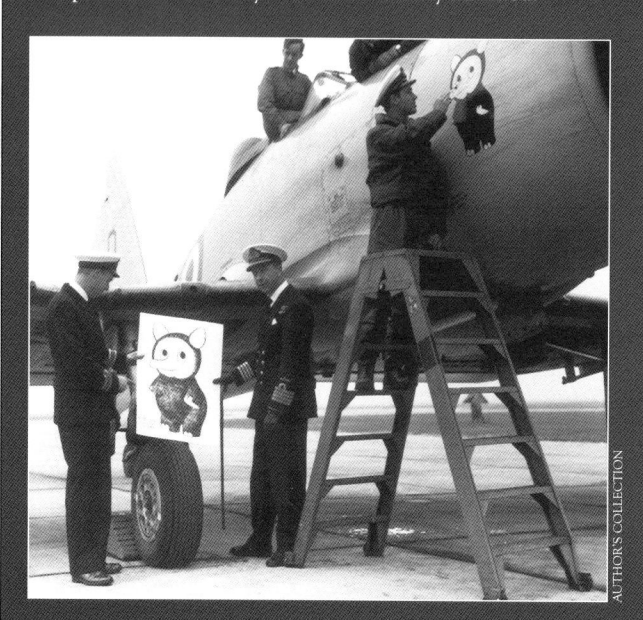

SHIPS AND SQUADRONS

Right: WN324 at Ford in 1957, painted up with the call-sign earlier applied to WN325 (see opposite). Bare RP rails are seen outboard beneath the wing, and practice bomb carriers can just be made out inboard.

Above: WP346—the final production Wyvern—makes a mess of both itself and two 804 Squadron Sea Hawks on board *Ark Royal* off Gibraltar in February 1957. The Sea Hawks, recently flown in from Hal Far, are still wearing their black and yellow 'Suez stripes', having earlier served on HMS *Bulwark* in the 1956 confrontation (when they also carried the tail code 'O').
Left: 831 Squadron officers in 1957: (front row, left to right) Lieutenant Doust, Lieutenant-Commanders Wheatley, Farquhar (CO) and Swithinbank (SP) and Lieutenant Cohead (AEO);(back row, left to right) Sub-Lieutenants Newton and Smith, Lieutenants Hartwell and McFall, Sub-Lieutenant Edward, Lieutenant Moore and Sub-Lieutenant Lutter.

FIFTY-FIVE

SECOND-LINE WYVERN SQUADRONS

Unit	Dates	Commanding Officer(s)	Remarks
700 Naval Air Squadron	18/08/55–00/02/57	Lt-Cdr R. W. Turral (18/08/55) Lt-Cdr D. G. Halliday (16/01/56) Lt-Cdr P. M. Lamb (23/01/57)	At Ford. Trials and Requirements Unit. Normally two aircraft on strength.
703W Flight	04/010/54–00/08/55	Lt-Cdr S. J. A. Richardson	At Ford. Holding unit for 827 NAS.
764 Naval Air Squadron	00/05/55–00/02/57	Lt-Cdr D. F. Battison	At Ford. Type conversion unit.

continued on page 61

Above: VZ782 of 703W Flight prepares to depart from *Ark Royal*, July 1955. This particular aircraft was originally assigned to 813 Squadron—indeed, what appears to be that unit's emblem can just be made out on the forward fuselage before being used by the Flight, and although, as with all 703's aircraft, theoretically earmarked for 827 Squadron, in the event it eked out its days ashore, ending up as an instructional airframe.

Below: VZ799 in 'retirement' at the Naval Aircraft Holding Unit, RNAS Lossiemouth, 1958, still wearing the emblem of 764 Squadron on the starboard forward fuselage. The spinners and forward portion of the engine cowling have been covered against the elements, and auxiliary intakes and outlets have been taped over. A close scrutiny of photographs of Wyvern S.4s reveals how individual aircraft—even those from a common production batch—differed in the arrangement of the intakes and outlets along the forward fuselage.

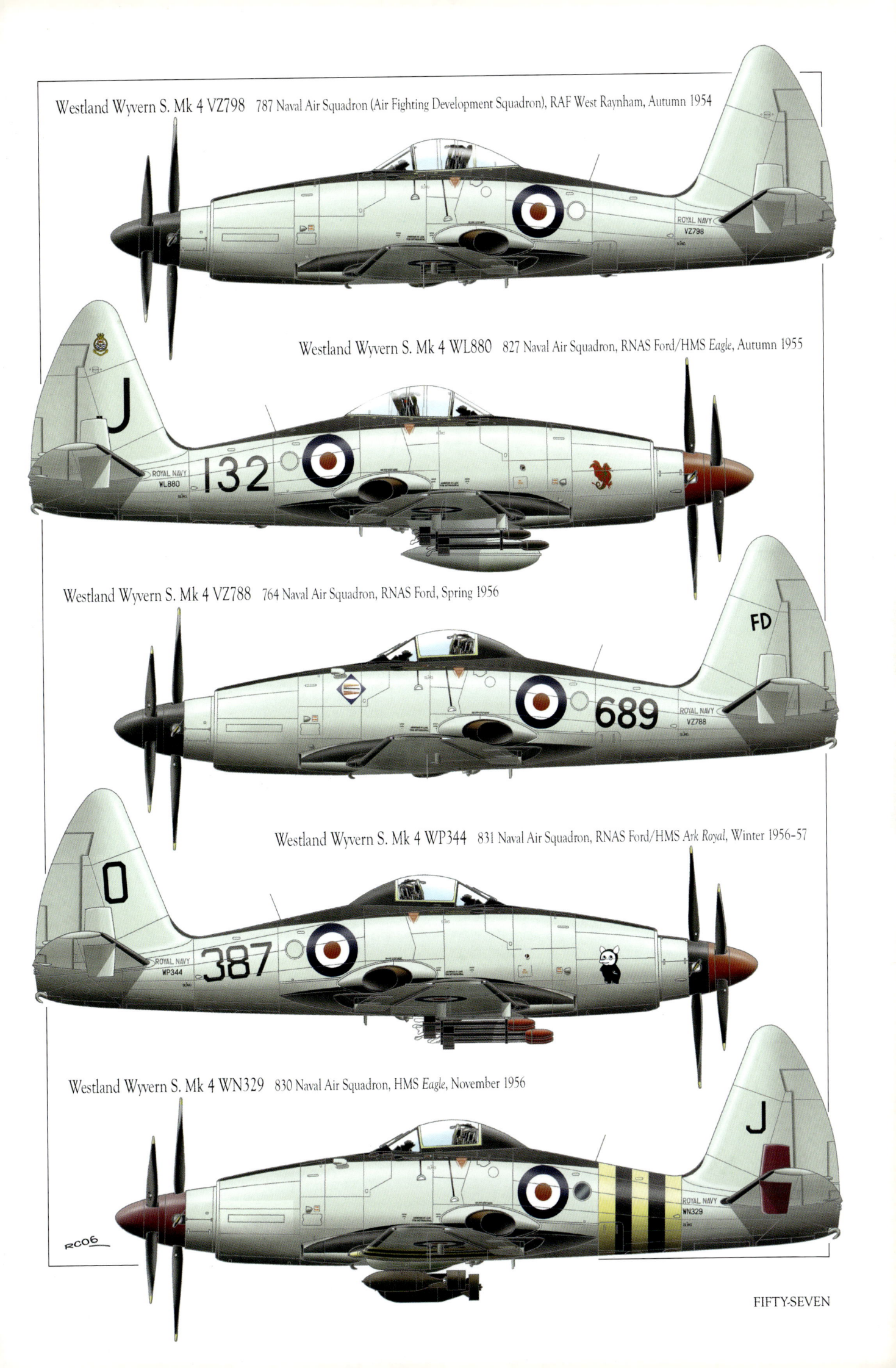

Westland Wyvern S. Mk 4 VZ798 787 Naval Air Squadron (Air Fighting Development Squadron), RAF West Raynham, Autumn 1954

Westland Wyvern S. Mk 4 WL880 827 Naval Air Squadron, RNAS Ford/HMS *Eagle*, Autumn 1955

Westland Wyvern S. Mk 4 VZ788 764 Naval Air Squadron, RNAS Ford, Spring 1956

Westland Wyvern S. Mk 4 WP344 831 Naval Air Squadron, RNAS Ford/HMS *Ark Royal*, Winter 1956-57

Westland Wyvern S. Mk 4 WN329 830 Naval Air Squadron, HMS *Eagle*, November 1956

FIFTY-SEVEN

WYVERN

FLOWN BY THE AUTHOR

FIFTY-EIGHT

SHIPS AND SQUADRONS

Westland Wyvern S. Mk 4 VZ789
831 Naval Air Squadron, HMS *Ark Royal*, Summer 1957

FIFTY-NINE

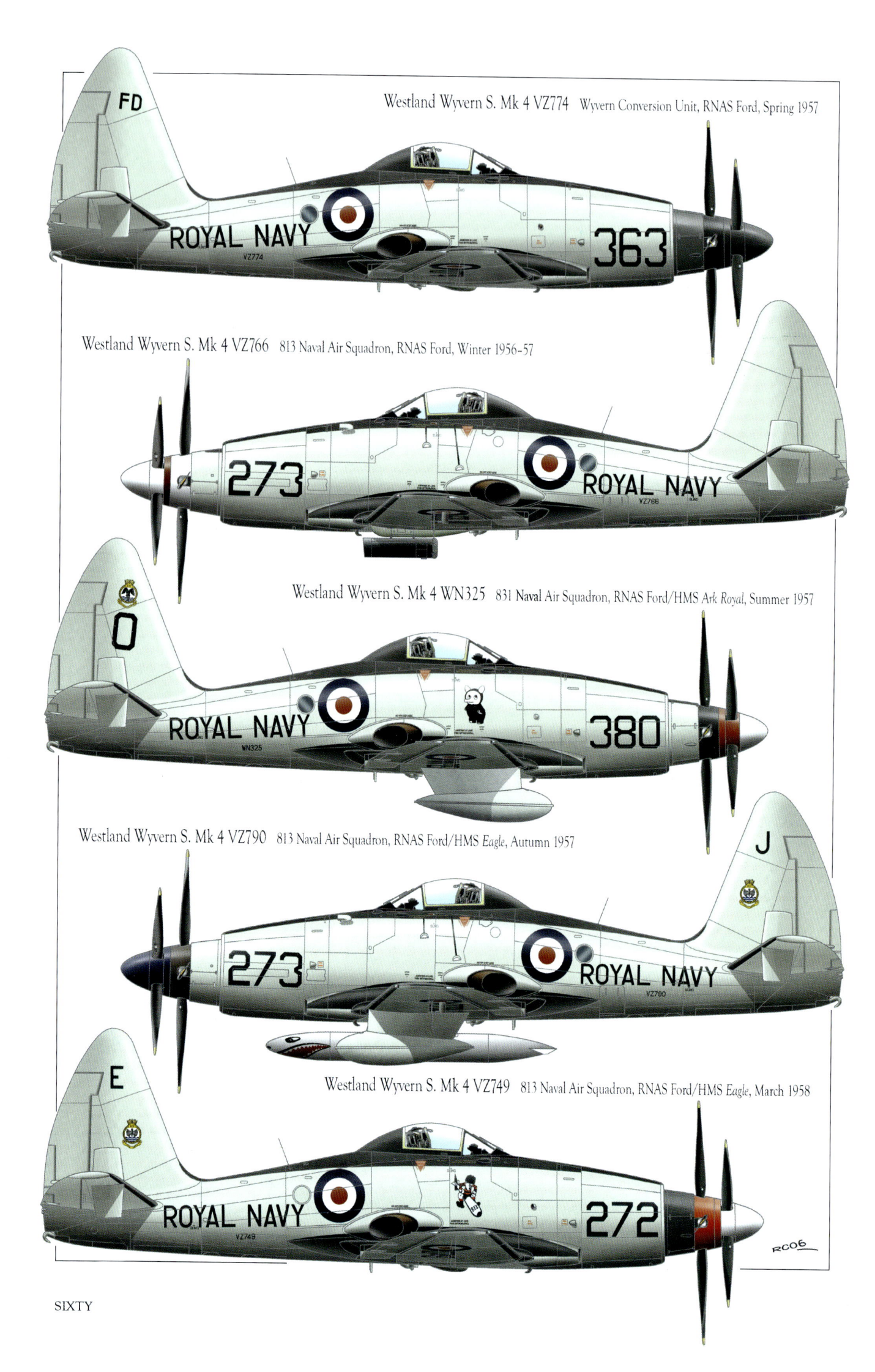

Westland Wyvern S. Mk 4 VZ774   Wyvern Conversion Unit, RNAS Ford, Spring 1957

Westland Wyvern S. Mk 4 VZ766   813 Naval Air Squadron, RNAS Ford, Winter 1956-57

Westland Wyvern S. Mk 4 WN325   831 Naval Air Squadron, RNAS Ford/HMS *Ark Royal*, Summer 1957

Westland Wyvern S. Mk 4 VZ790   813 Naval Air Squadron, RNAS Ford/HMS *Eagle*, Autumn 1957

Westland Wyvern S. Mk 4 VZ749   813 Naval Air Squadron, RNAS Ford/HMS *Eagle*, March 1958

SIXTY

SHIPS AND SQUADRONS

SECOND-LINE WYVERN SQUADRONS *continued*

Unit	Dates	Commanding Officer(s)	Remarks
787 Naval Air Squadron	00/03/54–00/11/54	Lt-Cdr R. A. Shilcock	Naval Air Fighting Development Unit, RAF West Raynham.
Wyvern Conversion Unit	00/02/57–00/12/57	Lt-Cdr D. F. Battison Lt-Cdr D. T. McKeown (17/06/57)	At Ford. Evolved from 764 NAS.

Right: VZ774 of the Wyvern Conversion Unit, at Ford in 1957. Wyverns permanently shore-based at that station were normally—though not invariably—coded 'FD'.

Left: VW886 of the WCU late in its career, with the revised style of markings alluded to on page 58. The tail code on this Wyvern has been painted more or less 'parallel' to the ground rather than aligned with the aircraft's horizontal datum. This variation in presentation was evident on other Wyverns of other units—front-line and second-line—as can be seen from the photographs elsewhere in this book.

Right: A slowly deteriorating VZ762, a former WCU aircraft, parked amongst other Wyverns at the Naval Aircraft Holding Unit at RNAS Lossiemouth, *circa* 1958, following the type's withdrawal from front-line Fleet Air Arm service.

SIXTY-ONE

'MUSKETEER'

I N NOVEMBER 1956, Egypt seized the Suez Canal, nationalised and closed it. Consequently, Britain and France went to war, and HMS *Eagle* found herself, together with two other British carriers (*Albion* and *Bulwark*), launching air operations against the Egyptian armed forces. As a result, 830 Squadron became embroiled in the hostilities, conducting armed missions against various Egyptian targets. This would be the one and only time that Wyverns would be engaged in combat. In the meantime, 831 Squadron and *Ark Royal* were placed on twenty-four hours' notice to deploy to the Mediterranean, in the event of any escalation.

Main image: Egyptian oil storage tanks burn following a strike by 830 Squadron Wyverns during the first week of November, 1956.

Above left: Yellow-and-black-striped Wyverns ranged aboard HMS *Eagle* just prior to taking part in Operation 'Musketeer'; all the diagonal 'finlet' stripes (seen here on '373') and aircraft call-signs would be painted out prior to actual operations. Two 897 Squadron Sea Hawks are visible at the top of the photograph.

Above right: Naval air power at its height: HMS *Eagle* steams at speed in the Mediterranean just prior to the outbreak of hostilities, Sea Venoms are ranged on the catapults and amidships, with Sea Hawks further aft and the Wyverns of 830 Squadron at the stern.

SIXTY-THREE

SEWING HALF-SOVEREIGNS
Lieutenant-Commander George W. Barras MBE RN (RETD)

HMS *Eagle* returned from Naples and on 29 July 1956 the Captain addressed the ship's company and gave advance warning of problems ahead, following Nasser's nationalisation of the Suez Canal. On sailing, we continued exercising and I was able to get back to flying practice in the Wyvern. We continued with round-the-clock flying, followed by another break in Malta. It was during this period that we lost one of the Sea Hawks during night flying. The pilot, John White, was lost. He was one of my original Cadet Term, the third one to go after Pete Beers in a Vampire at Lossie. After sailing, we carried out flying and amphibious exercises, and then did some joint exercises with the French Navy, during which several of their Corsairs carried out DLPs aboard *Eagle*. At the end of the cross-deck operations, we visited Toulon, berthing near the French carriers *Arromanches* and *Lafayette*.

After Toulon we continued training, including weapon attacks on Filfla, and mixed exercises with the RAF. It was about this time that Stan Roddick and I were involved in an air-to-air photograph which received quite a lot of publicity. The aim was to get a photograph of a Wyvern in the act of firing a salvo of 3-inch rockets. After a bit of planning and practice, a good shot was achieved.* We were also training with heavier weapons, and were carrying and dropping 2,000lb bombs, as well as sorties with three 1,000lb bombs—quite a load. One of the aircraft's limitations concerned its ability to carry mixed loads. In addition to the standard 20mm cannon, there were three weapon stations, which as stated could carry three 1,000lb bombs. However, the two wing stations were also the points for carrying the drop tanks, so a choice had to be made. Additionally, if drop tanks were carried, the number of rocket rails was limited. This meant that although a fair mix of weapons could be carried, there was a trade-off between range and load. Towards the end of the Wyvern's service life Westland were experimenting with the fitting of Venom tip tanks to reduce this problem, but it was too late for the aircraft.

For the next couple of months we continued to operate in the Malta area, carrying out strikes, weapon drills, night flying and exercises with the Army. In company with HMS *Albion* and *Bulwark*, we carried out a 'Balbo' over Malta, and then, in the middle of October, we sailed west to Gibraltar for a few days. With the nationalisation of the Suez Canal by General Nasser, there was a lot going on politically at this time, but, shielded in the ship, the likes of myself had little knowledge of the momentous decisions being made. However, by the end of October it was obvious that things were hotting up. We exchanged the Gannets for another squadron of Sea Venoms, 893, and the bombing practices we had been carrying out in recent weeks took on a new significance.

Finally the aircraft were painted with yellow and black invasion stripes and the aircrew were put in the picture, briefed and kitted out with khaki clothing, personal weapons and escape packs. We spent some time sewing half-sovereigns into our flying kit, and learned to strap on a loaded .38 revolver. At 0130 on Wednesday 31 October 1956, the Fleet switched off navigation lights as it approached operating area 'Alpha', about 330 degrees, 95 nm from Port Said, and flying operations started at 0240 on 1 November.

Action started at first light, and I was on the first Wyvern strike. Our target was the runways of Dekheila airfield at Alexandria, using 1,000lb bombs. The initial run inshore was a nervous time, with little knowledge of what air opposition there might be, compounded by some French Avengers in the area, whose position we did not know. In the event, the attack was virtually unopposed, and it was repeated twice more that day. I was on the last sortie as well, and we encountered some light flak on that occasion. Top cover during the attacks was provided by Sea Hawks from 897 and 899 Squadrons, also from *Eagle*. On Day 2, the first Wyvern attacks were again directed towards Dekheila, but my first sortie that day was against Huckstep Camp, an old British Army base some twelve miles south-east of Cairo and now a major Egyptian Army storage and transport base. For this attack we again used 1,000lb bombs. There was a fair amount of flak, and I had a hang-up. The return track was at low level over the Nile delta,

Below left: 'To Nasser with love': senior maintenance ratings pose beside a Wyvern on board *Eagle*, the aircraft's 1,000lb 'present' and port wing-fold mechanism evident. Messages scrawled on the bomb include 'From Stokes', 'Farouk' and 'Nasser sphinx's he's safe'. A rudimentary 'sharkmouth' has also been added, as has an 'ear', the latter accompanied by an explanatory label.

Below right: Bombing up a Wyvern for a raid over Egypt. The legend 'F20' scribbled at the noses of the 500-pounders refers to the type of fuse installed.

Above: Wyverns from 830 Squadron, painted in 'Suez stripes' and each carrying a single 1,000lb bomb and a pair of drop tanks, prepare to take off from HMS *Eagle* for an attack on Egyptian targets. The assertion—frequently encountered—that RATOG (Rocket-Assisted Take-Off Gear) was employed by Wyverns during the Suez Crisis can be dismissed: former 830 personnel have no recollection of such being used—or used, for that matter, by any other Wyvern squadron throughout the aircraft's career. Fitting RATOG to Wyverns appears to have been an idea that was tried out, but one that died an early death in the aircraft's development history.

and I was a bit worried with a higher than normal oil temperature, but got back to the ship in good order.

On Day 3, the main target for the Wyverns was changed to Gamil Bridge, and again I was on the first and third waves. For the first strike a single 1,000lb bomb was carried, but on the later strike we each carried three 1,000lb bombs. The bridge was on the coast, and destroying it would prevent reinforcements from coming along the coast road when the landings were carried out on Gamil airfield. The bridge was a solidly built stone structure, carrying both rail and road links, and proved to be very resistant to damage. It was during one of these attacks that Dennis McCarthy's Wyvern was hit by flak. He managed to drop his bombs and turned out to sea, where he successfully ejected and ended up floating in his dinghy some three miles offshore. Coastal batteries started to fire at him, until they were silenced by the Sea Hawk CAP. After being in the water for something over an hour, he was picked up by the ship's SAR Whirlwind flown by Pete Bailey.

The nights were a nervous time, with Egyptian destroyers and gunboats known to be about. One night the whole fleet lit up with all normal steaming lights, and made like the US Sixth Fleet, which was also in the area! Day 4 was a stand-down for HMS *Eagle* for replenishing. A spare Wyvern had been positioned at El Adem in Libya, and I volunteered to collect it. I was ferried there in one of 849's Skyraiders, and was back aboard by mid-afternoon.

On Day 5, the airborne assault was carried out on Gamil airfield by Hastings and Valettas dropping 600 paratroops of the 3rd Battalion. The Wyverns were tasked with troop support, but initially we were lacking ground control. Again I flew on the first and third waves against targets on the coast, the first against the coastguard barracks and AA guns with 1,000lb bombs and RP, and the second again with 1,000lb bombs, but with eight RP. It was during the second of these attacks that the SP, 'Smokey Cowling', was hit in the engine, and, losing power, he was unable to make it back to the ship and had to eject some twenty miles short. Again the ship's SAR came out, flown by Jimmy Summerlee, and he was picked up none the worse.

On Day 6, the last day of operations before international pressure caused a cease fire, 830 again flew three waves, all cab-rank sorties in support of the ground forces on the outskirts of Port Said. I flew on the second wave, armed this time only with ten RP and the standard 20mm cannon. Attacks were called by ground controllers, and it was rather like bees around a honey pot with the numbers of aircraft waiting to be called in.

HMS *Eagle* had done very well throughout 'Musketeer', having during the six days of operations flown 650 sorties—and all of this with only the port catapult operational. Following the ceasefire, *Eagle*, in company with the rest of the fleet, pulled clear of the area, but we remained at a high state of alert. The carriers were stood down in turn, and on 9 November *Eagle* returned to Grand Harbour for four days to replenish and to repair the catapult. On completion we sailed back to the Port Said area for patrols over the Canal Zone whilst the Army withdrawal was under way. The ship returned to Malta again at the beginning of December when the squadron had a final disembarkation to Hal Far . . .

* See pages 34–35 of this book.—Ed.

BATTLE 4 FORMATION

Lieutenant-Commander Robert King MBE RN (RETD)

By October of 1956 *Eagle* had arrived in Gibraltar on the way back to home waters, but we were immediately ordered back to Malta post-haste to take part in the Suez operation—which, appropriately for my two colleagues from flying training and me, was called Operation 'Musketeer'.

Before sailing for Suez, 812 Squadron's Gannet AS.4s were put ashore as it was considered that there was no role for them to play in the operation, and in their place we embarked a second Sea Venom F.A.W. Mk 21 squadron, 893 (which really belonged to *Ark Royal*'s air group but she was in refit at that time).

On the first morning of 'Musketeer' the first bomb ever dropped in war from a Wyvern was sent down by 'Vyv' Howard, our CO, and—typically of the man, who was never one to do anything by half measures—that bomb hit right in the centre of the intersection of the two runways at Dekheila, the airport at Alexandria, effectively putting it out of action for the duration of the operation. The significance of this was that Dekheila was home to the principal maintenance unit of the Egyptian Air Force, where Russian MiG fighters were assembled and test-flown after being shipped in. Those MiGs that had not left for Syria were, therefore, trapped and some were subsequently thought to have been destroyed by further Wyvern bombing sorties, in one of which I took part.

On looking through my Flying Log Book, I find that I flew on eleven operational missions at Suez. The most memorable of these was an attack on an arms and transport depot at Huckstep Camp, which was quite a long way inland. We flew in 'Battle 4 Formation' at about 15,000 feet so that we would have sufficient range for the sortie. This seemed to be entirely the wrong altitude for the AA guns: there was quite a lot of gunfire but none of our aircraft was badly hit, although a couple did sustain light damage. The return to the ship was carried out at extreme low level along the Nile delta, and I shall for ever remember the terrified look on the faces of Egyptian villagers as they gathered their children for safety. Those who have heard a number of Wyverns together at low level and high speed will know what a frightening sound they made.

On the fourth day of operations *Eagle* withdrew from the immediate area to carry out a RAS (Replenishment at Sea). Although we out of the operating area, all aircraft were fuelled and armed, in order to be available for action in the shortest time possible. In the forward section of the lower hangar two Wyverns were lashed down and in the centre section were four Sea Venoms. As Eagle was manœuvring to take station on the replenishing tanker, one of the 20mm cannon of a Venom started firing semi-armour-piercing and (high-explosive rounds which hit the drop tank of one of the Wyverns (it happened to be the CO's aircraft), the tank exploded and a major fire broke out.

The fire curtains were immediately lowered and sprinkler system for the forward lower hangar was automatically activated. However, before the cannon stopped firing SAP and HE had gone through a bulkhead into a mess deck and on the way had set off just about every alarm system within the ship. The situation was very serious, but well-trained officers and men, acting in the finest way, brought the situation under control very rapidly. The accident cost the life of one naval airman armourer, and a ship's company petty officer was badly injured. It could easily have resulted in the loss of the ship.

'Musketeer' was very short-lived, but before it was completed two more of our Squadron were shot down and had to eject. One of these was Lieutenant-Commander W. H. ('Smokey') Cowling, our Senior Pilot, who was hit by surface-to-air gunfire over mainland Egypt and, losing power and altitude, ejected some 50 miles from the coast, to be recovered by the ship's SAR Whirlwind. The other was Lieutenant Denis McCarthy ('Fred 8'), who also was hit by AA gunfire whilst bombing Gamil Bridge on the coast road just to the west of Port Said. Denis ejected quite close to the coast—so close, in fact, that the gunners turned their attention to his rubber survival dinghy. All was well, however: the guns were silenced by a flight of Sea Hawks and he too was rescued by *Eagle*'s Whirlwind.

HMS *Eagle* was in the last convoy to leave Egyptian waters in December 1956. After Christmas Day at sea she disembarked 892's and 893's Sea Venom FAW.21s and then called into Malta briefly to disembark the squadron ground crew, eventually arriving in the South-Western Approaches on 3 January 1957. Some of our aircraft were flown to RNAS Culdrose, some to RNAS Stretton and I flew ashore to Lee-on-Solent as No 2 to the CO—and so ended my association with the 'mythological' Wyvern.

Left: Wyvern WP338—piloted by 'Fred 6'—flirts with *Eagle*'s deck edge following a not-quite-textbook landing. Mediterranean, mid-1956.

RECOLLECTIONS OF A PLUMBER—3

Commander John Dunphy RN (Retd)

After 830 Squadron re-embarked it started working up in readiness for the forthcoming Suez conflict and the flying rate was increased significantly with the emphases on weapon sorties and night flying. We moved up to Toulon and commenced exercises with two French aircraft carriers. We stood off Toulon and started early in the mornings, flying sorties throughout the day and carrying on until 11 p.m. to midnight. The French carriers adopted a more leisurely routine and steamed out of port each morning at about 9 a.m. and joined us for exercise before returning to port at about 4 p.m. On the last night of the combined exercises we entertained a group of the French officers for drinks in the Wardroom and to watch our night flying activities. We asked them whether they were impressed with our flying efficiency. They replied in the affirmative but said, 'We cannot understand why you are doing all this flying at this rate, because you will wear all your aeroplanes out before hostilities commence!'

The aircraft had been painted up with black and yellow stripes for identification purposes and the aircrew had been issued with combat uniforms, handguns and escape packages containing silk maps and gold coins. Hostilities commenced on 31 October 1956. Wyverns attacked shore targets along the Egyptian coastline, damaging road and bridge communications, putting airfields out of action and destroying enemy aircraft on the ground.

The Squadron lost two aircraft. The Senior Pilot ('Smokey' Cowling) was hit by ground fire during ground attacks and he lost engine power and altitude on his way back to HMS *Eagle* (see photograph on page 27). He ejected safely and was picked up by the SAR helicopter and returned to the ship. Lieutenant McCarthy was hit by ground fire whilst diving down on his target and his propeller lost a blade which sailed over the top of his canopy. He power-zoomed up as high as he could, pointed the aircraft out to sea and ejected safely when he was a few miles off the coast. He landed in the sea and sat in his one man dinghy waiting for the SAR helicopter to arrive. A shore-based battery of Egyptian artillery then started shelling him with their 4-inch guns. The SAR pilot said afterwards that he found McCarthy sitting in his little dinghy surrounded by mighty water spouts, but he was picked up and returned safely to *Eagle*. It is interesting to note that the aircraft serviceability increased significantly during the period of operational flying and that many fewer defects were reported by aircrew. The words of the French officers at Toulon were prophetic as the engines and propellers in four or five of the Squadron aircraft became 'life expired' and flying only continued because they were given Emergency Life Extensions.

After hostilities ceased the invasion fleet anchored off the coast of Egypt, rectifying wear and tear on ships, aircraft and catapults. Aircraft were still struck down to the hangars with guns loaded and bombs attached in case of further enemy activity. One afternoon in late November an armourer was working on a Sea Venom aircraft in the Lower Hangar and removed the safety unit from a cannon. Suddenly the gun started to hose shells around the hangar. A couple hit a drop tank on an adjacent Wyvern, which exploded and caught fire. The armourer ran, but unfortunately he ran in front of his aircraft and was killed. The shells also punctured the hydraulic lines to the safety services in the hangar and the situation became rather tense. Off-duty members of the ship's company and Squadron personnel were ordered to muster on the flight deck and two destroyers came alongside in readiness to take off personnel should the need arise. In the event Fire Parties managed to contain the fire to the Lower Hangar and finally extinguish it. Thus ended the part(s) that HMS *Eagle* and 830 Squadron played in the Suez Crisis.

The carrier then prepared to return to Britain for repairs and to fly off the squadrons to disband. When we returned I was appointed to join the Director of RN Aircraft Research and Development (Lewis Boddington) in the Ministry of Supply (Aviation) in St Giles Court, London.

Below: The fire-ravaged WN336/'372-J' after being brought up to *Eagle*'s flight deck. The wreck was disposed of in time-honoured fashion—i.e., by unceremoniously dumping it overboard.

SPECIFICATIONS
WESTLAND WYVERN S. Mk 4

Dimensions	Length overall 42ft 4in (12.90m).
	Wing span 44ft 0in (31.41m) spread, 18ft 0in (5.49m) folded.
	Height (tail down) 15ft 6in (4.72m) with wings spread, 16ft 5in (5.00m) with wings folded, 19ft 0in (5.79m) max. height during folding.
	Wheel base 14ft 5in (4.39m).
Weights	15,660lb (7,100kg) dry, 24,500lb (11,110kg) fully loaded, 22,660lb (10,280kg) fully loaded with drop tanks full.
Fuel	Main tank 67gall. (305l), fuselage rear tank 106gall. (480l), fuselage front tank 105gall. (475l) or 95gall. (430l) when dual electric generatoirs fitted, inner wing tanks (2) 29 gall. (130l) each, outer wing tanks (2) 95gall. (430l) each. Total internal fuel 526gall. (2,390l). Drop tanks (2) 90gall. (410l) each. Total fuel all tanks 706gall. (2,310l).

Armament

Fixed	Four Hispano Mk 5 cannon (200rds/gun).
External	Maximum external load 3,000lb (1,360kg) .
	Bombs: 500lb MC Mks 7, 10, 14; 500lb SAP Mk 5; 1,000lb MC Mks 6, 7; 1,000lb MC Mk 8 (wings only); 2,000lb AP Mk 4 (fuselage only; practice bombs (wings only).
	Depth charge: 250lb Mk 11.
	Torpedo: 18in Mks15, 17 (fuselage only).
	Rocket projectiles: 3in Mk 3, 25lb or 60lb head; Mk 3 flare head (wings only). Eight single-tier or sixteen double tier if no drop tanks present; four single-tier or six (outer double tier plus single inner tier) if drop tanks carried.
	Mines: A Mk 7* or 7**, parachute assembly No 9 Mk 5 or Mk 6 (fuselage only); A Mk 8; A Mk 9, parachute assembly No 13 Mk 6 or Mk 7 (fuselage only); O Mk 1 (fuselage only). All on special carriers.
	SCI: 250lb Type G Mk 5.
	Smoke and flame floats: 3½lb Mk 1 (wings only).
	Reconnaissance flares: 4.5in Nos. 1 or 2 Mk 1 (wings only).

Equipment

Navigational	ADRIS (Automatic Dead-Reckoning Indicating System): Air Mileage Unit AMU Mk 4, Air Position Indicator API Mk 2.
	Compasses: Mk 4B compass, E2a compass.
	Chartboard: Situated below gyro gun sight (GGS).
Operational	Radio: VHF Relay (ARI 5491), Beacon Homing (ARI 5307), Beam Approach (A 1271), 'Green Salad' (UHF homer), external intercommunications socket.
	Radar: Radio altimeter, IFF (AN/APX-1), Radar Range (ASV.16), Tail Warning System (AN/APS 13). Contacting altimeter.
Armament:	Gyro Gun Sight Mk 4E, G45 camera and recorder, F46 torpedo marking camera (interchangeable with G45), F24 camera or cameras, gun controls, RP controls, bomb controls, torpedo controls, flare container control, 'Window' launcher.
Miscellaneous	RATOG and catapult gear, bomb/torpedo/external fuel tank jettisoning gear.

Performance

Max. speed	333kts (383mph, 616.6kph) at sea level, 330kts (380mph, 611kph) at 10,000ft (3,000m).
Initial climb	2,350ft/min (715m/min).
Service ceiling	28,000ft (8,500m).
Max. range	790nm (910 miles, 1,465km)

Left: The end of the road? Well, not quite. A Wyvern in 827 Squadron markings, lacking elevators and with extemporary wing-hinge reinforcement, makes its way along the A37 (!) during a period of refurbishment by the manufacturer, some time in 1956.